Additional Praise for *Living Without Limits*

I have read many motivational books but few have had the impact on me as much as Judy Siegle's book *Living Without Limits*.

We all eventually will have to face discouragement, sickness, injury, heartbreak, and many other burdens of life. Reading Judy's book will help you through your tough times.

—*Dale Brown, Legendary Basketball Coach, LSU*

This excellent book accomplishes many things. It reflects the faith, character and positive spirit of the author. It also contextualizes the role of faith in one's life; and it engages the reader with concrete illustrations and factual questions. *Living Without Limits* is both readable and profound. I am pleased to commend it to a broad audience of readers.

—*Paul J. Dovre, President Emeritus*
Concordia College

Judy Siegle grew up in a home full of faith, love, and support. Her life changed dramatically following a traumatic car accident but her foundation of faith, love, and support never wavered. Judy's candid stories about her life and how she has learned to lean on Jesus will make you want to follow the advice she provides in her book.

—*Jean Driscoll*
8 time Boston Marathon winner

Judy Siegle's story is an inspiring take of triumph over adversity. Circumstances and setbacks haven't kept her from living a life without limits, and her book tells how you can live that way, too. Applying the principles she shares will help you do more, and importantly, be more. I recommend it.

—*Mark Sanborn, Past President of the National Sp̶e̶a̶k̶e̶r̶*
Association and Author of The Fred F̶·̶ ̶*
Work and Life Can Make

Dedication

This book is dedicated to my Mom and Dad, to Tim and Marci, Aaron, Ryan, and Sarah, and to Susan and Ross, Becca, Betsy, and Tessa—without your support, I would never have been able to live this life without limits.

Acknowledgments

Special thanks to Tammy Noteboom, Susan Vitalis, Kim Fletcher, Jenny Rick, Tara Radniecki, Lora Albrecht, Care Tuk, Maryanna Young, Mike Yuen, Jill Engelstad, Carole Inman, Karen Stensrud, Dave Kolpack, Joni Eareckson Tada, Laura Hager, Don and Susan Otis, Ruth and Ray Siegle, Dick and JoEllen Solberg, Janet Lindberg, and Dan Miller for offering their skills and suggestions with this book process. Thanks to MeritCare Health System for helping my dreams become reality. Also thanks to the many friends and family who added joy to my journey!

Living *Without* Limits

10 KEYS TO UNLOCKING THE CHAMPION IN YOU

JUDY SIEGLE

with Cindy Fahy

LIFE VENTURE PUBLISHING COMPANY LLC

FARGO, NORTH DAKOTA

Unless otherwise indicated, all Scripture references are from the Holy Bible, New International Version, © 1973, 1978, 1984 by the International Bible Society. Used by permission of Zonderan Bible Publishers.

Scripture references marked Living Bible are from *The Living Bible*, © 1971 by Tyndale House Publishers, Heaton, Ill. Used by permission.

Published by Life Venture Publishing Company LLC
620 Main Ave., Suite 405
Fargo, ND 58103

Publisher's Cataloging-in-Publication Data
Siegle, Judy.

Living without limits : ten keys to unlocking the champion in you! / Judy Siegle ; with Cindy Fahy. – Fargo, ND : Life Venture Publishing Company LLC, 2005.

p. ; cm.
ISBN: 0-9766206-0-X
ISBN13: 978-0-9766206-0-0

1. Quadriplegics—Rehabilitation. 2. Quadriplegics—Religious life. 3. Self help techniques. I. Title. II. Fahy, Cindy.

RC406.Q33 S54 2005
362.4/3—dc22   2005-921804

Book production and coordination by Jenkins Group, Inc.
www.bookpublishing.com
Interior design by Debbie Sidman
Cover design by Chris Rhoads

Printed in the United States of America
09 08 07 06 05 • 5 4 3 2

Contents

Foreword

Before You Begin...

It's not often that I see quadriplegics standing, but Judy Siegle is one of them.

She was standing—a tad shakily—on stage at the front of the dining hall at one of our Joni and Friends Family Retreats. Dressed in her athletic garb, tanned and smiling, she looked like she could drop to the floor and do 50 sit-ups...lead us all in an hour of aerobics...or pick up a tennis racquet and smack a ball over our heads. That's when I noticed her hands. They were a little like mine—fingers curled and slightly "flat" in a funny way. I realized then that Judy's disability was probably more of a challenge than she was letting on.

My "fellow quad" inspired a lot of people with her story that evening. I watched her the rest of the week, hanging out with teenagers under a tree, parking her chair next to a kid over at the snack-shack, and counseling with parents about their child with spina bifida. No matter how late I wheeled back to my cabin, there was Judy with energy to burn, always hob-knobbing with a few night-owl volunteers. It would have been enough for her to invest her time like that at *one* JAF Family Retreat, but she kept showing up at others throughout the entire summer.

The lady's amazing.

Judy writes the way she lives. If she tells you she's got 10 keys to unlock a champion hidden away somewhere, you can bet on it. You would know that for sure if you had been sitting with me in the stadium in Sydney, Australia, when I cheered Judy on in her race in the 2000 Paralympics. My friend may not have come away with a gold medal, but you'd never have known that from the smile she flashed when she wheeled up to find me in the stands. Judy never seems to let a disappointment keep her from looking on the bright side.

When disability struck Judy Siegle, she discovered some incredible life-changing keys to character development and peace of mind. More importantly, she found wonderful keys in the Word of God. As a result, she discovered the "champion" within her, and she's never looked back.

In *Living without Limits,* Judy shares her warm and deeply personal journey, showing us how to see the potential for change and possibility in our own crazy circumstances. No, you probably won't learn how to smack a tennis ball over anyone's head, but you will find that champions come in all shapes, sizes, and ages. And, hey, you may find that you're a champion, too. As you read the life story of this extraordinary woman and observe the way she lives like a champion for Christ, you will discover that God has put no limits on *your* potential in Him. Just turn the page, open your heart, and take the keys in your hand...

There's a lot in your life to be unlocked.

Joni Eareckson Tada
Joni and Friends International Disability Center

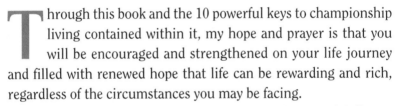

Preface

Through this book and the 10 powerful keys to championship living contained within it, my hope and prayer is that you will be encouraged and strengthened on your life journey and filled with renewed hope that life can be rewarding and rich, regardless of the circumstances you may be facing.

I have come to see that everyone has challenges of different sorts in life. Challenges are part of the universal experience of living. While we may not have a choice about the challenges that come our way, we do have a choice as to how we will respond. In these pages you'll discover principles that will not only maximize your potential—even in the midst of your challenges—but will find ways to discover joy, support, encouragement, and spiritual strength for your journey all along the way.

This is not a theoretical book of random principles. In my darkest days, I learned to apply these very specific tools, putting them into practice, living them personally. Each life principle is illustrated through my life story, which is woven throughout. Journal entries provide a glimpse into my mind and heart along the way, and bring clarity to the process of working through challenges.

At the end of each chapter you'll find Questions for Life that will help you incorporate these key principles into your own life story. For those who wish to go further in either small groups or personal reflection, a "Digging Deeper" section is included at the end of the book for your study. Scripture passages are provided to illustrate and support the use of the keys.

These 10 keys have brought hope to my days, energy to my body, mind, and spirit, and helped me to discover laughter, joy, renewed vision, and wonderful new sources of support. Through them, my own major life change was transformed from a tragedy into a gift that has opened my life to experiences and possibilities that never would have been mine otherwise.

Are you struggling to work through a time of transition or challenge or seeking to discover greater meaning and potential in daily living? This book will unlock and unleash the potential within you, freeing you to experience each day with a strong sense of purpose and to live with expectancy as you reach out to purposefully achieve your dreams and goals.

As I share my story with you, my hope is that you will come to realize that you are not alone on your journey: God wants to give you resources, strength, and tools to live victoriously. The keys that enabled me to overcome the challenges in my life can be your keys as well. Let me share them with you so you, too, can *Live without Limits.*

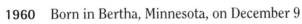

Timeline

1960   Born in Bertha, Minnesota, on December 9

1963   Family moves to Pelican Rapids, Minnesota

1979   Graduation from high school
Summer employment at Fair Hills Resort
Car accident on August 11, 1979
Hospitalized three months at St. Luke's Hospital (currently MeritCare Health System) and three months at Craig Hospital, Englewood, Colorado

1980-'84   Concordia College, Moorhead, Minnesota
Worked at Fair Hills Resort the summers of '80-'82

1983   Summer camp counselor at Red Willow Bible Camp, Binford, North Dakota

1984   Graduation from Concordia College with a BA degree in Speech Communication/Theater Arts

1984   Started graduate school at Minnesota State University-Moorhead in Speech Pathology

1985   Summer internship in speech pathology at Grand Forks Medical Center—switched to social work in the fall. Took social work classes at Minnesota State University-Moorhead that year while application processed at University of Minnesota, Minneapolis

1986 Began graduate school at the University of Minnesota in social work

1987 Completed coursework for MSW in December, 1987

1988 Began work at St. Luke's Hospital on January 4 as a psychiatric social worker

1989 Recognized as Fargo's Outstanding Employed Handicapped Citizen

1990 Recognized as North Dakota's Outstanding Disabled Citizen

1991 Transition to social worker on the rehab unit at St. Luke's hospital

1992 Started playing quad rugby and downhill skiing and attended a sports camp for people with disabilities in southern Minnesota. Ordered my first racing wheelchair.

1993 Started wheelchair racing

1996 Paralympics, Atlanta (4th place in 400 and 800 meter events, 5th place in 200)

1997 Set national records in 400, 800, 1500, and 5000 meter events for quadriplegic women

1998 World Games in Birmingham, England (4th place in 200, 400, and 800);
Traveled to Romania with Wheels for the World

1999 Para Pan Am Games, Mexico City (1st place in 400 and 800, 2nd in 1500);
MeritCare becomes official Olympic sponsor in support of me and changes my job to half-time social worker, half-time athlete/ambassador

2000 Paralympics, Sydney, Australia (5th place in the 1500, 6th in the 800)

2001– Present Community Relations Specialist for MeritCare Health System

The Game Begins

I never saw it coming. My boyfriend Dean and I were driving home that warm August night in 1979 after attending a wedding in southern Minnesota. Because it was a long drive home, we'd decided to get on the road early and had left the wedding dance before it was over. Dean was tired, so I'd taken the wheel of his '74 Impala while he slept.

Life was so good! I was 18, had just graduated from high school, and was eagerly awaiting my freshman year at Concordia College in Moorhead, Minnesota. My summer job at Fair Hills Resort near my hometown of Pelican Rapids, Minnesota, was a blast and my relationship with Dean was lots of fun. Yes, life seemed right on course.

Shortly after 1:00 a.m., a car full of kids who had been drinking came like a speeding bullet out of nowhere. Flying through a stop sign at excessive speed, they were trying to beat me through the intersection. I was told I hit their car broadside, but I have no recollection of the accident at all.

Two passengers in the back seat of the speeding car were dead at the scene, while the driver and front passenger were treated and released. Dean and I were both ejected from our car. Passersby called the police and we were taken to St. Luke's Hospital in Fargo, North Dakota, 45 miles away.

At 3:30 a.m. the phone rang at our family's lake cottage. Mom was there with my 16-year-old sister Susan and cousins Julie, Mike, and Katie. The caller identified herself as a nurse from St. Luke's Hospital and asked Mom if she were alone. Mom was petrified, knowing the news she was about to receive could not possibly be good. "Which one is it?" she wondered. Dad was staying in Thief River Falls, Minnesota, on his summer job as a crop hail adjuster, my brother Tim was visiting friends in Fargo, and I had gone to the wedding with Dean. It could have been any one of us.

"Judy has been in an accident and you must come immediately," Mom remembers the nurse saying firmly. Hearing the panic in Mom's voice, Susan promptly awakened.

"You can't go to the hospital alone!" she said. Susan ran to our lake neighbors and pounded on the door. Bryan Brierley drove Mom to St. Luke's Hospital and Susan called Tim in Fargo, telling him to hurry and meet us there. Meanwhile, the hospital called Dad, who immediately began the long drive to Fargo.

At the hospital, Mom and Tim, who was 20 at the time, were taken in to see me. My face was swollen—as round as a basketball—and splattered with blood. "Jude! Jude!" Tim cried at my bedside, but there was no response.

• • •

"Mrs. Siegle, I wish there was an easier way to tell you this," said Dr. Koski, the neurosurgeon. "Your daughter has sustained permanent nerve damage between the fifth and sixth cervical vertebrates. She has no voluntary movement in her arms and legs. She is going to be paralyzed from the chest down."

Word of the accident spread quickly throughout my home community of Pelican Rapids. At church the next day, the congregation prayed for me and grieved together. It was impossible to imagine such a tragedy. Having lived in Pelican Rapids since I was three, many of those in church that morning had been my teachers in Sunday School, choir, and confirmation class. Many had cheered at my basketball games, had attended my band concerts, and had watched me grow up.

Years later, as these same friends and family attended a send-off rally to the Paralympic Games in Atlanta, they would marvel once again at the amazing turn of events. And, full of promise and hope for what was to come, I would join them in their wonder.

The Paralympics? The second largest sporting event in the world, for elite athletes with physical disabilities? I never saw that coming, either, but here's where it all began...

● ● ●

On December 9, 1960, in the wee hours of that freezing cold morning, high school football coach Al Siegle took his toddler son Tim to the neighbor's house and carefully drove his expectant young wife, Faye, to Thiel Hospital, the small rural medical facility in the heart of the farming community of Bertha, Minnesota. The Siegles had recently settled in Bertha, population 470, where Al had taken his first job teaching social studies and coaching the Bertha-Hewitt Bears football team.

At 9:00 a.m., just as Al was settling in to watch *The Today Show*, the attending nurse interrupted his thoughts with the news that he was the father of a healthy, nine-pound, three-ounce baby girl. With a headful of auburn hair, baby Judith Kaye entered the world like a champ. She was big and beautiful—a perfect combination of her strapping, athletic father and her lovely mother. Oh, how proud they were of this robust baby girl!

Married just three years at the time, Al and Faye's little family blossomed in the tiny, close-knit community of Bertha, where neighbors were like family and friendships lasted a lifetime. Little sister Susan followed baby Judy two years later, and the Siegle family was complete.

Populated by teachers, farmers, and shopkeepers, Bertha's main street boasted a bakery, creamery, feed store, bank, grocery, and funeral home. It was a town much like Garrison Keillor's fictional Lake Wobegon, a town where character was deeply ingrained, where honesty and personal integrity were the marks of success. Here, the Siegle family formed a foundation of faith and love that would prove to be unshakable, and the seeds of a champion were planted in the heart of a little girl destined to overcome the unthinkable and to live a life without limits.

When I was two years old, Dad got the job as head football coach of the Vikings at Pelican Rapids High School in west central Minnesota. A bigger school than Bertha-Hewitt, this was a great opportunity for Dad, and Mom and Dad were very excited about the move to "the big city" of Pelican Rapids, population 1,835!

Those were wonderful years growing up in Pelican Rapids, where my elementary school days were filled with piano lessons, Bluebirds and Campfire Girls, backyard games like "Kick the Can" and "Fox and Geese," sledding on the big hill across the alley, Sunday School and church on Sundays, singing and acting in the school plays, choir practice, and football and basketball games. "Family Night" was always the highlight of the week, complete with colored popcorn, games, and watching westerns long after our bedtime. *The Shakiest Gun in the West* starring Don Knotts was our hands-down favorite!

Growing up, our house was a hubbub of activity. Initially, we lived three blocks from school in a small one-story house with a big backyard and a great climbing tree, swingset, and playhouse. Across the alley behind our house was the perfect hill for winter sledding. In sixth grade we moved several blocks away to a bigger house, where Susan and I had our own bedrooms—hers was light blue, and mine was yellow and orange with shag carpet. Our home was often a gathering place for friends, and on "storm days" when school was called off due to bad weather, this was where we played card games and royal rummy for hours on end.

Indoors or out, we invented our own fun. One of my friends, Karen Huseby, had a sister who was incredibly creative and we organized a carnival in our backyard to raise money for muscular dystrophy. Two summers in a row we put on this backyard fundraiser, complete with booths, skits, songs, and food. The neighborhood kids all came, and we proudly presented the proceeds to the Muscular Dystrophy Association.

During the school year Dad was a football coach, athletic director, and teacher. On Friday nights the town of Pelican Rapids turned out to watch the Vikings in action. I remember cheering the team on during those crisp fall nights, watching the cheerleaders perform their exciting routines and stunts to the roaring of the crowd, and dreaming of the day when perhaps I would be one of them.

Every fall Grandpa and Grandma Siegle from Montana joined us for a week to take in a football game. It was always extra special to have them with us, cheering Dad and his team to victory. With less distance to travel, Grandma and Grandpa Solberg came more often from Finley, North Dakota, to enjoy the football season and other school activities as well.

In the summers, Dad worked as a crop hail adjuster, traveling throughout the Midwest. So, every June, Mom, Tim, Susan, and I moved out to Pelican Lake to the family cottage that Grandpa and Grandma Solberg had bought for Mom and her brother Dick and his family. Dad joined us on the weekends, and there we spent lazy summer days swimming, boating, water skiing, living in our bathing suits, and building tents out of beach towels and blankets. Grandpa and Grandma Solberg came to the cottage every weekend loaded down with chocolate chip cookies, brownies, and fried chicken. Uncle Dick, his wife JoEllen, and their kids also were also a part of summer lake life. Thanks to an abundance of close, ongoing family connections and inter-generational contact, our childhood was filled with a strong sense of identity, unity, and belonging.

Pelican Rapids High School spanned grades 7-12, and during those years I became involved in everything I could possibly fit into my schedule: band, choir, ARA (Athletic and Recreation Association), speech, and drama. Naturally outgoing and adventurous, I ate up every opportunity to connect with people while embracing new skills and experiences. Mom and Dad provided that safe environment in which to try. We were never criticized at home because the expectation was that we would do our best and they would be proud regardless of the outcome. My first gymnastics meet as a seventh grader is a great example. I thought I would be good at vaulting because I had strong legs. In my first vault, I scored a 1.35 out of a possible 10, which was as low a vaulting score as I'd ever seen! I was also shocked when two of my closest friends scored a .6 and a .9 respectively on their parallel bar performances. "How could we be so bad?" we wondered. It was upsetting for all of us, but we resolved to only get better from there. We had done our best and figured we certainly had room for improvement!

Although I was involved in many activities, sports were my greatest love. Throughout high school, I was a football cheerleader and ran track, but basketball became my major focus. As a forward,

I was named to the All-Conference Team in basketball for three consecutive years, 1977-1979, and was named to the Minnesota All-State team during my senior year. I planned to play ball at Concordia College in Moorhead, where my parents, aunts, and uncles had all attended. Throughout my childhood I'd attended Concordia homecomings and annual Christmas concerts with Mom and Dad, and although I looked at other colleges, Concordia had a strong women's basketball team and I was looking forward to playing for the Concordia Cobbers.

During these formative years, Dad and Mom instilled a strong work ethic in Tim, Susan, and me. In the summers I had a job at the Dairy Queen, while during the school year I worked very hard to balance all my activities with a heavy academic load. The hard work paid off! At graduation, I was named salutatorian of my class and received the award of "All Around Student" for outstanding leadership.

At home, we had a lot of fun as a family and that bonded us together. At the center of our family's love and commitment to each other was a strong spiritual foundation that gave meaning and purpose to our lives. Every morning at the breakfast table before we headed off to school and work, we had family devotions from the Bible and a Lutheran devotional, *Christ in Our Home*. From my earliest days, faith in God was a very real and important part of my life. We attended Trinity Lutheran Church, which had a strong youth program, and I spent summers going to Bible camp, canoeing in the Boundary Waters between Minnesota and Canada, and attending national youth conferences.

Looking back at our family life, I realize that Mom and Dad put a lot of trust in us. We knew their expectations were high. I remember Dad saying that if we were ever in trouble at school or with the law, we would also be in trouble at home, so we never bucked the system. Because of the trust placed in us, we did not want to disappoint them, or cause them to regret their confidence in us.

Dad was the primary disciplinarian at home, and he rarely had to say something twice to get us to behave. The rules were simple and we all lived by them: do your best, work hard, respect each other, and be responsible, fair, honest, and true to your word. If you're given too much change at the store, give it back, and if you can't say something nice, don't say anything at all.

Mom was the nurturer in our home, the kind of mom who would cut my toast in strips and bring me 7-Up in bed when I was sick. She prepared wonderful meals and special birthday cakes, and she was always there with brownies, a button sewn on at the last minute, and all the special "Mom" touches that made our house a warm and loving home. She was calm and steady, but she infused our lives with joy and energy. A morning person, Mom woke us with a cheerful "Good morning" and breakfast on the table. She even counted the beat with me as I practiced the piano many mornings at 6:30 a.m.

Throughout our childhoods, we could always count on Mom and Dad to be at our activities. At sporting events, piano recitals, band and choir concerts, plays, and church programs, they were always our biggest cheerleaders. They devoted their lives to us, and gave us the best of themselves.

The day after I graduated from high school in 1979, I began working as a maid at Fair Hills Resort to save money for my upcoming freshman year at Concordia. Located on Pelican Lake, the resort was staffed by college students. I was very excited to be part of that staff, and I particularly loved the idea of participating in the weekly hootenanny that the resort put on for the guests. That summer sped by, filled with new friends, boyfriend Dean, lake life, and morning runs before maid duty. I even participated in the Miss Northwest Pageant with two of my friends in nearby Detroit Lakes, where I played piano in the talent competition and learned to walk in a bathing suit and high heels. I took fourth runner-up—not bad for a jock! Before I knew it, August had arrived.

On August 10 I attended the wedding in southwestern Minnesota with Dean. On the return home, in a split second, a speeding car turned my life upside down and I awakened an incomplete quadriplegic. My neck was broken, and initially I was paralyzed from the shoulders down. However, because my spinal cord was not severed (that's where the "incomplete" comes in), some of the nerve fibers were still able to make connections. This meant I would have muscle function in some parts of my arms and legs but not in others.

Dean broke his collarbone, some ribs, and his ankle in the accident. He spent a short time in the hospital and fully recovered from his injuries.

For the first several weeks after the accident, I was confused. At that time, the doctors called it a concussion, but today it would be known as a mild, traumatic brain injury. I remember not knowing how old I was, where I was from, or who the president was. At the hospital, every new shift of nurses would ask the same orientation questions all over again, and Mom would repeat the answers with me over and over, hoping I would retain the answers. I have vague recollections during that time of my brother and his friends coming from Concordia to visit me. Later they told me that I winked repeatedly at one of his friends (who just happened to be very good looking) and told him to "Come back single!" I was obviously confused and not myself. This kind of flirtation was totally unlike my personality, but we have laughed about this incident many times since.

Gradually, my mind cleared. My family had already had two to three weeks to process the news that I was now a quadriplegic, with arm movement only in the major muscles but no hand function or muscle return from the chest down. By the time I was fully aware and the details of the accident had become clear to me, my family was strong and able to help me process the enormity of the change that had taken place in my body.

Thankfully, my belief system did not change after the accident. Even though I realized I had undergone a huge change, I leaned upon the same beliefs I'd had before the injury. I was the same person on the inside and I knew that God was going with me through the struggle ahead, just as He always had. In the days ahead, however, I would learn more about this God of my childhood, about His character, His strength, His purpose, and more about the depth of His love than I could ever have possibly imagined.

About five weeks after the accident, the movement in the fingers of my left hand came back within one week—one finger each day—and the toe on my left foot began wiggling about three weeks later. In church that Sunday, our pastor thanked God for toes that wiggle! Weeks later, more muscles in my legs began to move. Unfortunately, only part of the muscles was getting the message, although we didn't know that at the time.

When I was moved to Craig Hospital to begin rehabilitation, relatives and friends who lived in Denver were great supports to me. I also called my family members or Dean just about every night because I had some down days. Alone and miles away from the supports I'd known, I looked forward to the mail and nightly phone calls that kept me close to my loved ones. My relationship with Dean continued to develop and he joined my family during their Christmas vacation for a visit. I also enjoyed the company of other patients, and I regularly wheeled myself to their rooms at night to hear their stories and learn what had brought them to this place in their lives.

I particularly remember watching the 1980 Winter Olympics from my hospital room at Craig and seeing the U.S. Hockey team take the gold medal. I was thrilled and proud of the United States. At that time, I never would have imagined that one day I would have the opportunity to represent my country as a world-class athlete in those very games.

Even though the days at Craig were hard, I pushed myself in therapy. As an athlete, I was trained to work hard and give my best, and I brought the same mindset to my "training camp" at Craig. I gave my all, just as I had given my all on the basketball court. That meant I eagerly participated in individual therapy sessions and group mat exercises, where I had the opportunity to physically push myself. This athletic training wasn't a new experience for me, just a new arena. Being "coached" was a positive, familiar relationship for me, and I thrived on the challenges the therapists put before me. I particularly loved the "endurance runs" on the sidewalk trails around Craig. My wheelchair at that time had "quad pegs" on the push rims. These pegs, projecting out from the rim, allowed me to push with only limited use of my hands. I also ate up the chance to relearn to cook, write, and dress myself with one-handed techniques, knowing these skills were preparing me to survive in the real world that I couldn't wait to rejoin.

My hard work began paying off. At Craig I progressed to the point of walking six feet with my first leg braces, a walker, and a therapist at my side. Although I gained more strength and coordination with the limited muscle movement in the years that followed, my walking continues to be very labored and effortful. Today I walk daily for my workouts at parallel bars and to a limited degree in my home setting, holding on to walls and counters, but the manual wheelchair is still my primary means of mobility.

I returned home from Craig in March of 1980 and began a session of summer school at Concordia College in May. Away from home and newly released from rehab, I wanted to see what it would be like to go to school in a wheelchair, so I started with one four-hour class in the morning. I soon realized that I needed a power chair. Because I didn't have the muscle strength at that time to push myself everywhere I needed to go, I was totally dependent upon my roommate to get around. It was an exhausting but exhilarating time, and I spent the afternoons studying and napping to stay in the game. I was relieved and rewarded when I received my first "A" in the college course that summer.

Once summer school ended, Fair Hills Resort welcomed me back. They put up ramps, made a cabin accessible for me, and put me to work in the store answering the phone and doing bookwork. I got my power wheelchair out there and participated in the hootenanny, doing just about everything everyone else was doing. Life was good—I had a job, friends, my relationship with Dean, and I was once again getting back to real life. The game was starting to get interesting again as I pressed past the limits of what I'd thought I'd be able to do.

I started college officially as a freshman that fall and graduated four years later with a degree in speech communication/theater arts. With a fresh diploma and a heart full of dreams and faith, I was firmly back in the game, playing to win. I would learn to use the tools that God had given me in my young life to craft a life of greater meaning and purpose than I'd ever dreamed possible.

At the time of the accident 25 years ago, I never would have imagined that today I would be speaking nationwide as a Community Relations Specialist for a healthcare organization. 25 years ago I never would have expected that I would hold national records in four events in wheelchair racing and that I would have competed in two Paralympics. 25 years ago, I never would have expected that I would travel overseas to Romania to deliver wheelchairs. But 25 years ago I did have hope that life could be full and good again.

This book chronicles that journey of faith. It contains my story, the story of the people God put in my path, the lessons they taught me, and the keys He gave that allowed me to rise above my circumstances and unlock the door to a full and joyous life once again.

Chapter 2

Meet Life Fully!

D uring the weeks and months following my accident, I was totally dependent on others to meet my daily needs. I had to be turned every two hours, fed, transferred from bed to wheelchair, and dressed and groomed. Yet the questions I found myself asking centered primarily around what was possible: "Can I still go to college? Have children? Drive a car? Travel?" Every question was met with a resounding "Yes!" This left me to conclude that I could live my life fully, even from a wheelchair. With a firm support system, a faith foundation, practical tools to move ahead, and a mindset firmly focused on the many opportunities before me, I ventured out.

For those who think a quad with a venturing spirit might be indulging in a bit of denial, let me underscore an important truth for anyone moving into uncharted water: we must always assess our possibilities through the 20/20 lens of reality, with eyes that are wide open. Certainly a quad has limits and very real physical barriers. To deny those facts is not only ridiculous, but unproductive. But future possibilities are birthed and nourished by embracing an attitude that is willing to discover and work with the resources we have today, by giving our all to moving ahead, and to making choices based on an attitude and heart that says "I can!"

Life is an adventure! Some people live their lives passively, making do with whatever comes their way. I choose to see life as an active experience. Meeting life fully means working with what you've got, daring to venture, living with expectancy, and sometimes even reorganizing your life picture.

Work with What You've Got

During my years at Concordia, I was very involved with the campus organization called Fellowship of Christian Athletes (FCA). Even though my game had changed a bit, I still considered myself an athlete. One week during the summer following my senior year, I worked at a leadership camp for FCA. Each morning the girls were out for their morning competition, playing flag football, volleyball, and basketball. I remember cheering for the girls and longing to be out there with them. It struck me that I shouldn't dwell on what I couldn't be doing, but instead develop who I was and the individual talents and abilities I had been given.

We all have different gifts. None of us have the same muscle picture, mental capabilities, dreams, passions, friends, family, or co-workers. No one else has your unique story. No matter what devastating change or unexpected turn has come, no one can touch your world like you can. When you dare to venture out, using your own completely individual set of life tools, the impact can be significant—for you as well as those who will be blessed by your contributions.

Stay in the Game

While at Concordia, I kept the 30-second clock at the women's basketball games. As a former All-State basketball player in high school, I knew the game well. Keeping the clock meant I could still be part of the action. Occasionally people would ask me, "Doesn't it bother you to work at the games on the sidelines?" It may sound funny, but I didn't grieve that particular loss, because I had given my all while I had the ability and I felt good about that. Plus, while keeping the clock was a different experience than playing, there were still rewards from participating—getting to know the players, the excitement of the event, and using the ability and knowledge that I possessed. Operating the 30-second clock required only one hand, and it was a critical part of the game. To be an integral part of that sports environment brought me joy. The alternative was to avoid it altogether and miss out on the relationships, the opportunity to contribute, and the satisfaction of participating in something rewarding and exciting.

Years later, in the summer of 1995, as I was training for regional wheelchair racing competitions around the country, my friend Carole Inman invited me to be her partner in the Riverfront Days Triathlon coming up in Fargo. The three-part event would consist of biking, canoeing, and running. We strategized our game plan carefully: I would do the running portion of the race in my racing chair, Carole would do the biking, and we would canoe together. The previous year I had learned to canoe with the help of a stadium seat strapped to the canoe seat, while an adapted golf glove helped me hang onto the paddle. I would have the front position in the canoe and Carole would bring up the rear, to steer and keep us on course. Friends were arranged to carry me from the shoreline of the Red River to the canoe and help me transfer from the canoe to the racing chair.

Three hours, 15 minutes, and many sore muscles later, we took seventh or eighth place out of about eight teams, but as far as I was concerned, it was a sweet victory. I'd achieved my goal—to stay in the game, to fully participate, to engage in a new adventure, to stretch myself, and to discover the joy of meeting life headlong!

The alternative to full participation in life is restricting and paralyzing. Making a choice to be involved and using what we've got is not only freeing, it brings a sense of self-esteem, strengthening our self-perception while building our character for the next challenge ahead.

Dare to Venture

I lived in the freshman dorm, Hoyum, during my first year at Concordia, even though it wasn't wheelchair accessible. Although Concordia had a wheelchair-accessible upper-classmen dorm, it wasn't where I wanted to be—I wanted to be with the screaming girls and blaring stereos!

When I asked to live at Hoyum, Concordia's administration agreed, even though Hoyum, which has three steps down to its first floor, couldn't be ramped because of fire codes. This meant transferring from my power chair to my manual chair and asking people to take me up and down those steps several times every day. Was it always easy? No way! It meant more labor for me and was more exhausting, but the positives of the freshman dorm experience far outweighed the negatives. Best of all, my close high school friend, Lynn Kelting, was my roommate, and my cousin, Ann Siegle, was our dorm resident assistant and lived right across the hall. Throughout all the adjustments of a freshman year, they were my trusted supports and best pals, helping to pave the way for me into that new and challenging college world.

That first year, I went to bed each night earlier than most college students because I was wiped out at the end of the day. But in my mind, I was almost like every other freshman girl. I lived in the dorm, I had a full schedule of classes, I worked out daily, I had a boyfriend back home—I wasn't that different just because I was in a wheelchair. It was so important for my self-perception to see myself as a normal college freshman.

As it turned out, relying on others brought wonderful blessings my way. Because I needed help up and down those stairs, everyone in that dorm eventually became my friend—or at least they knew me. The girls, and even some of their boyfriends, learned how to manage my wheelchair, and I was included in all the dorm activities, including the brother-sister floor social activities. Yes, even panty raids were part of my experience, and I am so grateful for the opportunity to fully experience the joy of life in the freshman dorm!

I still had moments of grieving, however. There were times I would close my dorm room door and let the tears fall because it was hard. How I wished I could be there with a healthy body! Freshman orientation days prior to the start of the year were particularly poignant. I went to Gooseberry Park to participate in relays with the other kids and I choked up as I watched them compete. While my group leaders worked hard to help me participate in the events to the best of my ability, it just wasn't the same.

Crying released the grief I felt over these difficult moments. Often I would listen to a song by Evie Tournquist: "When I think I'm going under, part the waters, Lord. When I feel the waves around me, calm the sea."

"God, I'm goin' down," I would pray. "Lift me up!" The words gave me comfort and encouragement that reached down into the depths of my soul. Realizing He was going with me lifted me up. Even though hardship and grief are real, they don't have to hold us down or keep us from enjoying what is possible in life.

Keep Walkin' It Out

Sometimes life forces us to venture. After my accident, my family and I were thrown into a whole new world of disability, spinal cord injury, and wheelchairs. When faced with a significant change or challenge, an adventurous attitude keeps us moving forward towards a positive outcome. The alternative is to stay stuck in habits, routines, circumstances, or situations that hinder our development, stunt our potential, and limit our future. While venturing brings growth, it's tempting to stay inside our safe comfort zone because fears enter in—the fear of failing, the fear of what other people may think if we do things a little differently, the fear of the unknown.

After my accident, I dealt with the fear of falling. It was one thing for me to walk in the gym at Concordia for my workouts during my senior year, but it was quite another thing when the therapist I was working with said I had to start "walking in public." Although it rarely happened, I was terrified of falling while walking in public. At this point I had progressed to walking short distances with just a cane in my left hand. With my right hand paralyzed, I thought that I couldn't hold anything in that hand. My fear was great: if the cane hit water or a rock, I could potentially fall. Later on, I put a leather strap on the handle, fastening my right hand to the crutch, which gave me another point of balance.

Choosing to venture in spite of my fears, I plugged "walking in public" into my routine as a college student. Here's how I did it: I got around campus in a power chair, but when I got to class I would drop my book bag at my desk, park my chair out in the hall around the corner, and walk into class. On the positive side, I was standing, seeing people eye to eye. On the down side, I hated feeling so awkward and clumsy.

One weekend at home I had a heart-to-heart talk with my dad about the therapist's instructions. "Dad, I feel like a fish out of water when I'm out of that chair!" I said, in tears. "I can be myself in the chair—I'm comfortable and I know I'm not going to fall!"

Dad's response helped me to understand that it wasn't going to get any easier unless I made myself do it. That night I went to bed and took out my devotional, *My Utmost for His Highest,* by Oswald Chambers. On this particularly difficult day it said, "It takes almighty grace to take the next step when there is no vision from God [Where is this going, God? Why am I doing this?], no enthusiasm [I'd lost that long ago!], and no spectator [someone to take my hand—I would go anywhere if someone would take my hand]." Chambers went on to say that it takes a conscious drawing on God to take that step. Wow! I couldn't believe how clear God could be! He knew just what I was dealing with!

The next Monday morning I dropped my book bag off at my desk, parked my chair around the corner in the hall, and offered a prayer. I said, "God, I don't have the strength to do this, but you say to draw on you so here I am!" And off we went. I found that as I parked, paused, and offered that prayer, I began to overcome my fear of falling. I memorized Psalm 23 as a way to consciously draw on God to take that step. I would walk into a movie theatre or restaurant or a banquet at which I was speaking and I would say, "Here we go, God! Even though I walk through the valley of the shadow of death, I will fear no evil for you are with me. Your rod and your staff they comfort me." Over time I became more confident in my walking and I eventually totally overcame my fear of falling.

As Eleanor Roosevelt famously said, "You gain strength, courage and confidence by every experience in which you really stop to look fear in the face. You are able to say to yourself, I lived through this horror. I can take the next thing that comes along; you must do the thing you think you cannot do."

Learn That Falling Isn't Failing

I never fell in the classroom situation I just described, but I had to learn that falling wasn't failing; it was part of the process. It is in the attempt that we move ahead. As we move through life, we are going to fall and we are going to fail. Jean Driscoll, a fellow wheel-chair racer and eight-time winner of the Boston marathon (a feat never before achieved by able-bodied or disabled racers), with many Paralympic medals to her name, often says, "People think of failure as the opposite of success. How wrong! Failure is actually part of success." We can learn from our experiences and actually grow stronger as we get up and evaluate what went wrong, what worked well, and what we need to do differently to succeed.

As I developed the adventurous attitude of daring to step out, I believed God was speaking to my heart, encouraging me every step of the way. "Use what I'm giving you! So what if you're not always graceful. You have no idea what is possible with Me!" As I ventured out of my comfort zone, doors opened and opportunities came my way. What a thrill it was when those doors would open into the sports world once again.

Discover Doors of Opportunity

Early on as a quad, I thought my days in the sports arena were over. But, because fitness and sports had always been part of my life, I worked out daily, knowing how important it was for me to have as much strength as possible for the activities of daily living.

12 years after the accident, I heard about Wilderness Inquiry, a group that takes able bodied and disabled people on outdoor chal-lenge experiences around the country. With their help, I learned to canoe and kayak. Thanks to Ironwood Springs Christian Ranch and supportive friends, I eventually tackled downhill skiing, tandem biking, water skiing, and horseback riding as well.

Quad rugby was my first exposure to wheelchair sports in 1991. I was a social worker on the rehab unit at the time and the rec therapist, who was also a quadriplegic, asked me if I was inter-ested in joining the team. I played for the North Dakota

Wallbangers for three years and absolutely loved it! Quad rugby is played on a basketball court with a volleyball. It's a wild and wonderful experience and definitely not for the faint of heart, as chairs smash together and bodies fly! I was the only woman on the team and probably the last one off the bench, but it was such a thrill to be involved in sports again, doing the best I could with the muscle strength I had. I knew how important the bench was to the success of the team because I had been out on that court before.

At my first national quad rugby tournament in San Jose, California, I met several experienced wheelchair athletes from New York who introduced me to the world of wheelchair racing. "Judy, get into road racing!" they said. "Find out where the running races are in your area—chairs can race, too!" I wasn't sure there would be opportunities for wheelchair racing in North Dakota, but I came home from that tournament in San Jose pumped and ready to go! I ordered my own three-wheeled, lightweight, streamlined chair and started taking part in area races, traveling to Minneapolis to learn the sport and improve my skills.

As the world of athletics once again began to open to me, the wheelers in Minneapolis told me that to compete against other quad women, I would have to go to the national or international level of competition. The competitive athlete within me was coming to the surface, and I wanted desperately to know how I would do against other quad women! I had read about the athletes and sports program for people with disabilities at the University of Illinois in Champagne in a magazine called *Sports 'N Spokes*. I called the coach, Marty Morse, and told him I'd like to train with him. His response was immediate: "Come on down, Judy!"

That spring, a friend and I drove my car down to Illinois for a few days of training and later that fall I flew down for an intensive racing clinic. The talk and hype of the clinic was on making the U.S. Paralympic team in Atlanta in 1996. "Is this something I could do?" I wondered. I was thrilled at the possibility! When I was able-bodied, I never would have dreamed of being Olympic material, yet as a quad woman it seemed strangely—incredibly—within my grasp! I never dreamed new horizons would open to me as a result of being a quad, yet a future I'd never imagined possible seemed to be opening before my eyes!

At the training camp in 1994, at the University of Illinois, I watched the other wheelers and took notes on their training programs. To be a good wheelchair racer, muscle strength is important, but an athlete's position in the chair is crucial to maximizing every ounce of power with each push of the wheels. I'd been racing for a couple of years, so I thought I was doing pretty well. Then it was my turn to get on the "rollers," a type of treadmill for racing chairs, to get feedback from the coaches and trainers. After a hard workout on the rollers, they shared with me that my positioning needed some improvement and that I wasn't making the best connection with the wheels.

While these suggestions were given to me in a positive way and the adjustments were made, I got off the rollers and returned to my hotel room that night more than a little discouraged. I wondered if I even wanted to make the Paralympics. It sounded like a lot of work, a huge commitment, a pretty big sacrifice. Then I thought back to my college days and the lessons I'd learned from my struggle to walk...lessons about daring to step out, daring to take risks, daring to venture. That night I realized the truth: "I've got to try—whether I make the Paralympic team or not!" I knew it would be a positive experience just giving my all and putting myself out there. My prayer that night went something like this: "God, I don't know if the Paralympics are in your plan for me, but if they are, put the supports along the way to make it happen." God did answer that prayer, opening doors, providing all I needed, and making two incredible Paralympic experiences possible in my life.

Give Your All

When we give our all and do our best, we are winners regardless of the actual outcome. We might not win first place, we might not earn a medal, we might not even make it to the race. Still, much is gained from taking the opportunity to stretch ourselves and opening our hearts, minds, and bodies to growth and development. Daring to try expands our world. With every new experience we learn and grow simply by putting ourselves out there, making connections with others while setting and achieving goals. Venturing brings growth, opens our hearts and minds to new opportunities, and increases our vision.

In the 1996 Paralympics in Atlanta, I took fourth place in both the 400 and 800 meter events and fifth place in the 200 meter. In Sydney, Australia, in 2000, I took fifth in the 1500 and sixth in the 800 among a field of 14 quad women. I will never forget the honor and pride I had in my heart as I proceeded into Olympic Stadium for opening ceremonies decked out in my red, white, and blue to the roar of 120,000 fans. I will never forget living in Olympic Village and competing at Olympic Stadium while daily connecting with some of the best athletes in the world. I even had the wonderful opportunity of praying with one of my competitors. While I didn't bring home a medal, I was a winner simply by being there and doing my best. Venturing opened my world, deepened my faith, increased my vision, and catapulted me to heights I'd never dreamed possible. When we give our all, we experience enormous rewards even when the outcome might be a bit different than we expected.

Nancy Hogshead, the most decorated swimmer at the 1984 Olympics in Los Angeles, sums up the motivation and determination that sustained her through eight years of world-class competition, resulting in three gold medals and one silver: "Why push yourself? The answer: because the rewards of reaching for excellence truly are profound. I'm not talking about a pay raise, a plaque, or even a gold medal. It's living into a purpose or a calling that enlivens even the most mundane tasks. It's a deep pride in the life we are living...It starts with a daily commitment to the goal and continues with hard work, which is the underpinning of any achievement...Going up, down, and around obstacles is normal, something to be expected when pursuing a big goal...Expect the obstacles and embrace the struggle of growing."

Live with Expectancy

As Tim Hansel, author of *Holy Sweat*, says, "A new adventure explodes into being anywhere and anytime a person listens to God and faithfully obeys Him. That is the adventure like no other! It's a surprise-filled journey towards deeply knowing ourselves and the One who made us."

Living with expectancy means living in the moment—embracing it—knowing God is in full control. It means expecting God to fulfill His purpose in our lives even though it may be different than our own. Sometimes when life takes a detour, things don't appear to make sense. Anticipating God to reveal something fresh in those unexpected moments enables us to be at peace even when we don't understand, and gives us strength and courage to keep pressing on.

In 2003 I was traveling to Fort Wayne, Indiana, to speak at an insurance conference, and I ran into bad weather conditions at my layover in Detroit. I had to spend the night and get on a flight the next morning. The hotel shuttle driver who picked me up the next morning began sharing the hardships he was going through in his life. I don't know exactly what it is about a wheelchair that makes people open up about their personal hardships, but over and over again people seem to feel that because I use a wheelchair I will understand their pain and know what they are going through. This man was no exception. I heard him out and we shared together, and he was deeply encouraged by our contact and overjoyed that our paths had crossed. "I know the reason you're in my shuttle this morning," he said. "You were meant to be here for me!" If I had been totally focused on the upset in my schedule, I would have lost the opportunity to hear this man's story and would have missed the blessing God had for me...and him!

Sometimes life throws us into situations that are completely different from what we planned or intended. When we view life as an adventure and look for the "silver lining," deviations become opportunities for new relationships, experiences, personal growth, and a richer understanding of life and the impact we can have on others.

Repaint Your Life Picture

After my accident and rehab, many experiences were new and uncomfortable. With all the adjustments and transitions, I was mentally and physically exhausted. There was a sense of loss, of being different. I had to plan ahead and organize my new life, leaving behind old patterns and establishing new ones. Even my sense of identity had to change to fit new realities. For example, in high school I had been a basketball star. I had to rethink my life picture (or so I thought) without competitive sports as a part of it. Instead, I focused on getting my college degree, a goal that pushed me to overcome the obstacles in my path.

I really didn't have any role models to help me understand what a person in a wheelchair on a college campus would look like. At Concordia, I met with the college housing director to learn about my campus housing options. Considerations like getting to the dining hall, accessing my mailbox, and obtaining my books from the non-accessible campus bookstore were all issues I had to overcome. When I spoke to the registrar to discuss my class schedule, we realized that some of my courses had to be moved to accessible buildings.

Throughout the process, no one said "no" or questioned my ability, so I kept moving forward toward my goal of getting my college degree.

Once my freshman year began, there were many new situations that were uncomfortable and awkward, like having my roommate transfer me to a bath bench in the shower just for starters! Simply negotiating my daily schedule was physically exhausting because I was still getting used to a different, weaker body. Taking care of myself—dressing, applying make-up, and fixing my hair—were major feats to be accomplished each morning before I even rolled out the door.

Once in the classroom, I was well aware that I was different. I tape-recorded class lectures because my writing was slow with my left hand. The hum of the wheelchair went with me wherever I went, and I remember thinking that I was outside the circle, looking in. In high school I had been one of the leaders of the pack, involved in everything. Now I had to pace myself. I knew that one of my strengths was my sharp mind, so I poured my energy into my studies, and academics became my first priority.

Socially, a lot of students interacted at the Normandy, a kiosk-like snack bar. This wasn't accessible to me, so I rarely went there. Another common hang-out was the bar and dance floor in the basement of the Trader and Trapper Restaurant. I went there once and could be social in any environment, but it hurt me to go because I loved to dance. At that time, I wouldn't have been caught dead on the dance floor in my wheelchair, so I chose not to return.

In those college years, even when life didn't make sense and seemed terribly hard, I clung to my faith and the goals I'd set for myself. These gave me the determination to press on. I remember motoring my power chair across campus, and when I passed someone and caught myself lowering my eyes, I would say to myself, "Judy, hold your head high—God is going with you!"

With the passage of time, new routines aren't new anymore. As we master new behaviors and even a new environment, confidence replaces the old self-doubt and fear, enabling us to open new doors of opportunity with strength and courage.

Sometimes, however, the doors that open involve hardship and circumstances that aren't ideal, but propel us towards achieving our greater goal. Starting in my sophomore year, for three years I took classes in Speech Pathology at nearby Minnesota State University-Moorhead. This meant I had to take the bus system for people with disabilities—waiting hours on either side of my class for the next available ride. It was frustrating, inconvenient, and humbling, and yet it got me further towards my goal so I buckled down and did it.

Setbacks, new obstacles, everyday life challenges, and the ups and downs of living do not have to derail us. We can make a choice to keep moving forward through the barriers, even when circumstances have changed and the path towards the goal is entirely different than we had once dreamed.

We can still get there!

> **Obstacles to Overcoming: Why People Say "NO!" to Venturing**
>
> Day to day stress
> Loss of a loved one
> Loss of job/career
> Illness/Disability
> Divorce
> Financial hardship/risk
> Addiction
> Loneliness
> Depression
> Betrayal in a significant relationship
> Self-consciousness
> Lack of support
> Fear of the unknown
> Fear of failure/success
> Sacrifice of hard work

Sharpen Your Vision

We live out our lives in reference to our perception. During my years as a social worker and an employee assistance counselor with MeritCare, I occasionally worked with people who came from dysfunctional families or social systems that limited their growth and development personally and/or professionally. I came to understand that our present day experiences have been filtered through an emotional "lens" made up of past memories and experiences, both good and bad. This lens can cause us to see new events in our lives with an altered view, distorting our perception of what lies before us. What makes an obstacle an obstacle is our perception.

We can replace distorted thinking by turning away from the negative, dysfunctional patterns in our lives. When we realize that past patterns are destructive, painful, and are no longer working, we can make a choice to move away from the pain, sharpen our vision, and forge a new path. It takes courage and determination to walk away from old behaviors and patterns, but we do so trusting that we are moving ahead into health and opening to the fresh possibilities of each new day.

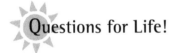

Questions for Life!

1.   What fears keep you from stepping out and meeting life fully?
2.   What would you do if you were ten times bolder?

C h a p t e r   3

Let Go of Stress

I do not remember my accident at all. Because I sustained a mild, traumatic brain injury, my memory of the entire event is simply erased, which I consider a blessing. As my memory gradually returned, I did not have the sudden blow of being able-bodied one minute and looking at life from a wheelchair the next. Instead, as I faded in and out of consciousness for two to three weeks, there was a gradual process of discovering what had happened and the new situation I was in. This time period allowed my family to go through that initial shock and grief at a time when I was not fully aware of what was occurring. By the time I was told about the accident, my family was adjusting to the situation and able to give me their full attention. They communicated to me loud and clear: we will deal with this together!

With this new realization, I immediately relied upon the same belief system I had before the injury. In my life up to that point, I had learned that God was going with me, so I naturally thought, "God's going with me here, too. Why should I be down?" At that early point, there was no way I could comprehend just how my life had changed, but my days were positive and filled with home-town support as I worked hard in therapy.

Understandably, however, I did go through struggles that came out at night with restless sleep and nightmares. Weeks went by and it eventually came down to one particular morning when the occupational therapist came in to exercise my hands, which weren't working at all yet. Just as she did every morning, the therapist tuned the radio to the broadcast of the Concordia College chapel service, where I was supposed to have been a freshman that fall. I began telling her just how badly I was feeling about my restless nights. With the sounds of the broadcast filling the room, my thoughts turned to Concordia—the kids, the books, the girl's basketball I was supposed to be playing. I broke down crying and knew I needed to talk to somebody who could help me process the reality of living life from a wheelchair.

Venting: The Healing Release of Emotion

I called Concordia's campus pastor, Ernie Mancini, who had been the speaker at my high school graduation just the spring before. He came over that night and told me there were going to be many more times when I would feel frustration, hurt, even anger at God. But if I could share those feelings with God, if I could vent and let out those feelings in a healthy way, if I could cry and be true to the depth of emotion going on inside me, then I could deal with those thoughts constructively. He told me to imagine God so close to me that I could beat on His chest with my anger.

That talk totally ended my nightmares. The next day I was back in therapy, and though no one knew anything was different, I knew I was not going this new way alone... God was going with me, just as He always had.

I did not fall into a major depression after the accident in part because I learned early on to let out my feelings in a healthy way. Whether it was talking to a friend, a family member, a counselor, or God, I was constructively releasing my emotion. Over time, however, I learned that grieving my injury and venting the loss of life as I had known it was not going to be a one-time event. The process would take place at different times, with different people, and sometimes when I least expected it. The emotion, loss, and change would fall fresh on me again, and I would once more allow myself to acknowledge the pain, to feel the range of emotions, and release them again.

Family members have unique ways of coping with the changes and challenges inherent in any major life event. When one of the members of a family system is affected by hardship, all are affected, and all respond differently according to their own personality and role within the family unit.

My mom is a verbal Scandinavian. After the accident, she felt she needed to be strong and supportive, yet she was torn up inside. Mom became adept at stuffing her emotions, putting one foot in front of the other each day, doing what had to be done. She was like a mother bear watching over her injured cub, not allowing herself to break or let down. Several years after the accident, I was speaking at an event and looked out into the audience to see Mom on the verge of tears. "Mom, what's wrong?" I thought. "I'm alive!" I didn't understand that she was still processing the loss of all she had hoped, dreamed, and prayed for in my life. Several years later she began having difficulty sleeping and knew she had to get some help. The doctor asked about my accident, and she broke down in tears, finally allowing herself to grieve.

My dad is a stoic German, and as the strong head of the family, he was a "take-charge" and goal-oriented person. I never saw him show any emotion after the accident. Yet, I'm told that my Uncle

Ray, Dad's brother and a pastor, had a service for our family in the hospital chapel the night after the accident, and at that time Dad allowed himself to grieve. After that, he took charge, led the family through this very difficult time, and was an anchor for us all. True to his style, he dealt efficiently and effectively with his emotions, put His faith in God, and moved forward.

My brother Tim, who is two years older than me and was a junior at Concordia at the time of the accident, came every day to the hospital to visit. It was especially meaningful when he sat with me on Sunday nights to do his homework after the rest of the family and friends had gone home. He stayed with me, quietly chatting and offering his gentle companionship, until I fell asleep. Although Tim was generally positive and upbeat, my accident was very emotionally and physically draining for him. He did cry after the accident, yet as a student with a full load of classes and a member of the football team, he needed to get on with his life. Much of the time he confessed his heart wasn't in his work and he felt as if he were simply going through the motions. By the time I left the hospital for rehabilitation at Craig, Tim was feeling so drained and sick that he finally went to the doctor and discovered he had a case of mononucleosis.

My sister Susan is two years younger than I am and was a junior at Pelican Rapids High School at the time of the accident. This should have been her time to be fully immersed in high school activities with Mom and Dad cheering her on. However, much of their time and attention was spent attending to my needs. Susan knew that if it had been she who had been injured, Mom and Dad would have been there for her, too. Even at her tender age, she recognized they were where they needed to be. Still, there were times when she felt their absence and grieved the circumstances that prevented their full involvement in her high school experiences. Thanks to our close-knit family and the community of Pelican

Rapids, relationships with friends and extended family helped to provide the support Susan needed at this time in her life.

My freshman year at Concordia, I remember closing my door on occasion and crying because of the loss I was experiencing. We had communion on campus on Wednesday nights and those were especially emotional times, not because I was asking "Why me, God?" but because I sensed His presence even in the midst of my hardship. Even so, there was a huge sense of loss. During that first year or two after the accident, I wondered if I would ever laugh really hard again. I sensed that I was different...that somehow things would never be the same again. Yet I learned that with time, as I vented those feelings to God, I could be healed by His grace and move on into all He had planned for my life.

During this critical time of adjustment, I was given a book on the life of a young woman named Joni Eareckson. Joni had become a quadriplegic in a diving accident when she was 17—before her freshman year of college—just like me. Her story was an incredible encouragement as she chronicled her journey from despair to finding joy and purpose in living.

In the years since her accident, Joni had become a nationally acclaimed mouth artist, best-selling author, radio broadcaster, and highly sought-after speaker, tackling tough questions we all deal with—issues of faith, suffering, and the nature of God. And through her organization, Joni and Friends, Joni had become a world-wide advocate for people with disabilities, touching lives and changing the culture of disability for countless thousands.

Needless to say, Joni lived each day with great faith in a great God. Even when her game changed, like mine had, she pressed on and allowed Him to take the pieces of her life and make something that would, in time, impact the world. Her life was a bright beacon of light to me, showing me how to navigate along a path few would ever travel.

During my sophomore year, Joni was invited to speak at Concordia and I had the wonderful privilege of introducing her to the crowd. Before she spoke, I spent some time alone with her, sharing some of my struggles to adjusting to life with a disability. Knowing Joni had dealt with the same issues I was facing, I trusted her as a source of wisdom and strength. She encouraged me to keep using what I had, and in her warm and down-to-earth manner and beautiful smile, I found renewed hope about the possibilities before me.

It would be four years after the accident before I grieved what I thought was the end of my participation in competitive sports. At that time, I didn't know about sports for people with disabilities. Though I worked out every day, a huge part of my motivation for workouts was to be able to walk normally throughout my day. I still didn't know what was possible in my walking, so it continued to be a strong priority and goal. Dad was my coach during the summers of my junior and senior years at Concordia. Our routine consisted of walking at parallel bars, swimming at the downtown pool, and doing mat exercises on the living room floor.

One morning Dad and I were finishing up with the morning mat routine of exercises and the last exercise was crawling on my hands and knees for endurance. When your coach says "endurance," you know you're going to hurt! I didn't like crawling one bit! This day I was crawling as Dad was commanding: "Forward! Backward! Forward! Backward! Faster forward! Backward!" On this particular day, though I was hurting physically, I was hurting so much more mentally.

Dad concluded the crawling exercise and the morning workout with, "That's it, Jude! Good workout!" I fell back exhausted and tears flowed down my cheeks. "I need a competitor, Dad!" I cried. "I need to know where I am in this race. If I'm in last place, at least I know how far I have to go. But I need a competitor!" Dad was a little taken aback by my outburst—that had never happened before.

He said, "You've got me and you've got Rocky, too!" (Our family dog never missed my workouts.) As much as it meant to have great parents and wonderful family support behind me—and yes, even man's best friend at my side—they couldn't know how I was hurting that morning.

I vented, the tears fell, and then it dawned on me that even though my family didn't know what I was going through, my God, in the person of Jesus Christ, knew just where I was at. He hung on the cross for me. What I was going through was nothing compared to what He went through for me. 1 Peter 2:23-24 says, "When they hurled their insults at Him, He did not retaliate; when He suffered, He made no threats. Instead, He entrusted Himself to Him who judges justly. He Himself bore our sins in His body on the tree, so that we might die to sins and live for righteousness; by His wounds you have been healed."

That morning I grieved again the loss this injury represented in my life, in particular the loss of competitive sports. As I did so, in some mysterious way, an energy returned to my body, mind, and spirit. The next day we were back exercising with as much gusto as ever—Dad, Rocky, and Jude.

Today my preferred ways of venting are my workouts and phone conversations with trusted family and friends. Some months I've opened my phone bill and have been shocked! All I can think is, "Wow! It must have been a high-stress month!"

I also have a daily prayer journal where I chronicle activities, concerns, fears, relationships, upcoming events, and organizations of which I'm a part, inviting God's direction and involvement in my life.

Such journaling was not a new process after the accident. I kept a diary in high school where I expressed some of the challenges of being a teenager. For example, in my junior year of high school, I wrote the following:

Feb. 26, 1978, my junior year of high school:

God, there is something inside me that is so uneasy right now and I don't know what it is. I've got so much on my mind; there's a dance in a couple of weeks and I think David is going to ask me. Sometimes I want to be with him and other times I don't, and I don't know my reasons either way and I'm scared about that. On Tuesday we go to that Math contest, of which I'm so afraid of completely blowing! Then there's track coming up and I think I'll go out because I love being involved, but I've no idea of what I could even half decently do and that scares me. And God, I have college on my mind a lot, too and I'm excited for it. Oh dear God, don't let me look to the future or worry so much about the future that I miss all the great, great happiness of today! And don't let me take for granted what I've got today for I am so truly blessed.

After the accident, it was natural for me to turn to journaling once again:

January 14, 1980, Craig Hospital, Englewood, Colorado

Mom and Dad called and we had a good talk. I told them how scared I was about reaching a plateau at some point, and Dad said, "Were you scared two months ago? You could have plateaud then. Don't worry about things you can't control." Oh, he's so smart! Although I haven't ever been this close to walking, he's right—don't worry about things that you can't control. So God, this is too much for me to handle. I put it in your hands!

February 18, 1980, Craig Hospital

Today was a really down day! I don't know why. I guess it had just built up. I went to mat class and afterward I just lay on the mat and thought, "Oh, I hate this! I wish I were normal! I had so much going for me..."

August 20, 1996, Paralympics in Atlanta

Lord, reduce the stress and anxiety I am feeling right now. Fill me with your spirit. Give me your peace. The race last night went fairly well. We were delayed by a rainstorm for one hour, which gave us a shorter warm-up time. The track was wet, so times were slow. I took first place in my heat with a time of 1:15.50. Father, keep me focused throughout the race tonight. These are finals for the 400. Help me to be mentally strong for whatever situations come up...

November 4, 1999, Para Pan Am Games, Mexico City, Mexico

Lord, we are just about off on another journey. It's 6:35 a.m. and I'm heading to Mexico City for the Pan Am Games. I've heard that our planes from Chicago to Mexico City have been canceled, so this should be an interesting day as we will all be arriving into Mexico City at different times. I could get overwhelmed—a foreign country, disabled, can't carry my bags, but I choose to trust you, Lord, and to see how you will work this out!

Journaling, putting down on paper what is going on in your heart and mind, is another form of venting and can make you feel better! A study conducted by North Dakota State University psychology professor Joshua Smyth and colleagues from State University of New York at Stonybrook showed that writing about a stressful experience reduced physical symptoms in patients with chronic illnesses. Smyth and his team monitored 112 patients with arthritis or asthma. Subjects were asked to write in a journal for 20 minutes three days in a row either about an emotionally stressful incident or their plans for the day. Of the group who expressed their anxiety on paper, 50% showed a large improvement in their disease after four months. Only 25% of patients who wrote on neutral topics showed any relief of symptoms.

Processing Change and Letting Go Gradually

Sometimes grief reactions to life-altering events can surface years after the event itself, triggered randomly by memories, chance encounters, activities, events, friends, or family. Any one of these can instantaneously propel us back in time to once again feel the pain of loss and grief afresh.

15 years to the week after my accident, I unexpectedly ran into Dean, my old boyfriend, at a church service. We had dated a couple of years after the accident but with college life consuming much of my time, we gradually drifted apart. Eventually I came to realize that God was moving us in different directions and I felt a peace about moving forward on my own. Dean had since married and had children and was living in California. He and his family were in the area for a visit and had arrived that Sunday morning shortly after my family. My heart was just pounding as I sat there, and I kept thinking during the service, "Judes, don't break down...God, help me not to break down." It was a communion Sunday and I walked with my crutches up for communion, thinking just how disabled I was with my halting walk.

At the end of the service we walked out and greeted Dean and his family. I asked him about his life in California and told him what I was doing. As we spoke, I began to choke up and the tears began to fall. We concluded our conversation and I went out to the car and just wept. Later, I went home and lay on the bunk in our lake cabin, grieving again what a terrible accident we had been in together. I wept for hours that day.

At 18 my life had been turned upside down and 15 years later things were vastly different than I would ever have imagined—I didn't have a husband or children, which I certainly had expected to have by that time. I vented my sorrow, the tears fell, and I was able to move on once again.

Changing Our Self-Perception

I was 28 years old and had been a psychiatric social worker at MeritCare for two years when I received a call at work that was going to rock my world and shake my sense of identity once again. The caller said I had been chosen as Fargo's Employed Disabled Citizen of the Year by the Mayor's Committee on Employment of People with Disabilities. My heart just sank. "No way! I am not disabled," I thought to myself. I was doing just about everything everyone else was doing and I didn't want to accept this award and all it implied.

I cried that night and asked myself the hard question: "Judy, are you having a hard time adjusting to your disability?" I certainly realized that I was disabled, but because I had never associated to any degree with people with disabilities, I had not assumed the identity of a woman with a disability. Maybe I was doing things a little bit differently, but was I really disabled?

Clarity came as I realized I needed to grieve again the changes that my disability had brought to my life. By the time I accepted the award from the city of Fargo, I was able to see it as a huge honor. In 1990 I was also named Employed Disabled Citizen of the Year by the Governor's Committee on Employment of People with Disabilities for the state of North Dakota. Little did I know how these awards would change my life and open doors I'd thought were closed to me forever.

At the state conference in Bismarck, our speaker, Kirk Bauer, executive director of Disabled Sports USA, talked about downhill skiing. A disabled Vietnam veteran, he became an outstanding skier and ski racer, winning medals in national competitions from 1972-1980. "I don't care what your disability is; you can ski!" he challenged us. I was thrilled by his words and excited beyond belief at the possibility of once again fully participating in a sport I'd grown up to love. "I'm going to ski, too," I promised myself that day, and indeed I did. An award I initially did not want to receive ended up being a life-changing blessing. My self-perception began to change that day as I began to see myself as a vibrant, healthy woman living in a world full of potential, possibility, and promise.

You might be curious about how a quad skis. I relearned this sport that I love in a sled that had two skis underneath it. My poles, called "outriggers," had a top like a fore-arm crutch, while the bottom of each pole had a mini ski attached that gave me stability and brakes. I skied tethered, by reins, to an instructor who skied behind me to help me control my speed. It truly was a phenomenal feeling to be out on the slopes again, and I will always be grateful for the opportunity to take part in this exhilarating sport!

Four Types of Stress

Stress of one kind or another is always with us in today's world. A stress-free life is most likely an empty, unproductive life. Four types of stress are defined below; the key is to learn to deal with stress in healthy, proactive ways so that it is manageable, and even a positive motivator, rather than damaging to our minds or bodies.

Eustress

"Good stress" pushes us to perform at higher levels. This is controlled, short-term stress that motivates us and gives us a competitive edge in activities such as athletics, giving a speech, or acting.

Distress

Distress occurs when the demands upon us are so great that they tear down our ability to function mentally and physically.

Acute Stress

The most common form of stress, acute stress is short term and results from the demands and pressures of the recent past and the anticipated demands of the near future, such as moving, changing jobs, experiencing loss, an accident, or work-related pressure.

Chronic Stress

Chronic stress is relentless and wears down the body and mind day after day. This includes the stress of poverty, dysfunctional families, and despised jobs.

According to an article in *Critical Care Nurse,* more than two-thirds of visits to doctors are due to stress-related illnesses. Psychologist Ray Oakley has found that more than half of all the deaths in the United States can be attributed to social and behavioral factors such as stress. Research in both medicine and psychology concludes that severe, ongoing stress contributes to the weakening of the immune system and increases the body's vulnerability to disease and illnesses such as asthma, arthritis, high blood pressure, and heart disease.

The American Academy of Family Physicians (AAFP) says there are other red flags that stress is getting the better of you: depression, nervousness, guilt, fatigue, headaches, stomachaches, insomnia, laughing or crying for no reason, or no longer taking pleasure in things you once enjoyed. Awareness of these physical and emotional changes is the critical first step to charting a more positive course.

Stress Switching

In *A Minute of Margin,* Richard Swenson states, "Unresolved stress has a way of usurping our attention and dominating our mood." When you have gone as far as you can with a project and are feeling stuck, it's time to take a break and direct your energy elsewhere. Swenson calls this "a stress switch." He writes, "Any kind of diversion representing a voluntary change of activity is often better than inactively ruminating on the stressor."

Examples of stress-switching activities could include reading a novel, painting, talking on the phone, gardening, or volunteering at the library. Even a short amount of stress switching seems to be beneficial. I like to use music to de-stress, as do many others. Swenson says it well: "When God created music, he somehow ordained that it would be able to penetrate through the multiple layers of our consciousness and go straight to the depths of our spirits."

At the Paralympics in Atlanta in 1996, track and field athletes had a two-hour bus ride just to get to the warm-up track. Most of us listened to music through headsets to occupy our thoughts, get the adrenaline flowing, and prepare our mental state for the competition to come. During the ride, I chose music to calm my heart, focus my mind, and remind me of God's presence. Lorie Line's piano collection of hymns did just that, lifting my heart and allowing me to focus my energy on the competition ahead, with no negative thoughts to pull me down. Gratitude to God for the experience and opportunity before me filled my heart as I listened to those beautiful hymns of the faith. At the time of the biggest competition of my life, at one of the largest sporting events in the world, stress-switching through the gift of music calmed and assured me of God's presence and prepared me for peak performance.

Additional Stress Busters

It's important to find healthy ways to let out that emotion going on inside:

1. In addition to venting and/or journaling, talk to your other supports: family members, friends, co-workers, neighbors, medical professionals, church family, those with shared interests, counselors, pastors, and teachers. (Developing this network of support will be discussed in Chapter 8.)

2. Exercise regularly: 20-30 minutes of physical activity benefits both the body and the mind. According to Karen Uhlenhuth in the *Kansas City Star*, "When the human engine is kicked into high gear, everything changes. The blood moves faster, the pulse and blood pressure increase, the chemical factories all over the body switch from producing compounds that can cause disease to compounds that promote health."

3. Develop hobbies: take a break by doing something you enjoy! Painting, quilting, gardening, working in the yard, learning to play an instrument, or reading can be healthy ways of letting out emotion.

4. Pray and meditate.

When we deal with stress in a healthy way, our energy is continually renewed and we rid ourselves of negative baggage. If we stuff our emotions, sooner or later they erupt. Be proactive! As we let stress go, we maximize our energy, renew our minds, and refresh our spirits. It's all part of living without limits!

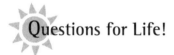

Questions for Life!

1. What stresses are limiting your life today?
2. Which stress busters do you typically use? Are they working?

Chapter 4

Cultivate an Attitude
of Impact

O ne of my favorite Paralympic memories from the games in Sydney in 2000 dealt with the positive attitude of a Paralympic volunteer toward two athletes from the tiny country of East Timor, located in Southeast Asia. East Timor became a country in 1999, just the year before, and this was obviously the first Paralympic team ever to be sent to the games.

One of the athletes, a polio survivor and power-lifter in the Games, walked with a tree branch for a cane. The other athlete was a runner with cerebral palsy. The athletes spoke very little English, had almost no money, and shared a small bag of belongings. The volunteer who was checking these athletes into the Paralympic Village was surprised by what he saw. There was little more than some old clothes and only very limited and outdated training gear.

He got on the phone immediately and spent hours phoning potential equipment and clothing donors, with amazing results. Within hours these young men were decked out in suits for the opening ceremonies, had competition and workout attire, and so much more. The story circulated through Olympic Village and throughout the world, and many who heard it jumped on board to help. The attitude became contagious, and the East Timor athletes probably had more fan support than any other athletes competing in the Games that year. All because of one man's attitude.

Change Negative Self-Talk . . . and Change Your Life!

It was Henry Ford who once proclaimed, "Whether you think you can or you can't, you're probably right." Our words have tremendous power to build up or to tear down either ourselves or others. I learned about the power of "self-talk" at a retreat I attended several years ago.

The different sessions focused on our self-talk and how to change negative internal messages to positive statements, giving us power and control in situations where we need them most. A critical part of understanding this principle involves writing out affirmations—positive statements that become the basis of verbal declarations to yourself concerning how you want your life to be. Positive affirmations are a great way to clear away negative thoughts; they support our efforts to build the lives we desire.

Negative thinking is actually very hard work! It drains our energy, causes stress, and can rob us of the joy of living. During graduate school, at Minnesota State University-Moorhead in 1985, I used positive affirmations to deal with important issues that affected the everyday quality of my life, including eating habits, walking, and driving. I didn't have a driver's license yet for driving with hand controls, but I was taking driver's training and beginning the process of getting back behind the wheel. The idea of learning to drive with a knob on the wheel for steering and using a lever off the steering column instead of my legs for acceleration and brakes was daunting! Also, I had been the driver in my accident years earlier, and I knew that driving again had the potential to be a dreaded and fearful experience. So, one of my affirmations to counter that negativity became the following:

> *"I enjoy the independence that*
> *driving my car gives me!"*

I also had developed some very bad eating habits, using eating as a way to cope and get through graduate school. Two of the affirmations I used to assist me in changing this destructive behavior were:

> *"I enjoy eating what is good for me"*
> and
> *"I enjoy stopping eating when I am full."*

Affirmations also brought a positive, optimistic approach to my daily workouts as I pressed on towards my goal of walking:

> *"I am confident in my walking and*
> *enjoy being outside of the chair."*

What we say to ourselves is what we will bring into being. These affirmations helped me to gain control of my life again, and the next summer when I did go through driver's training, I was thrilled to be behind the wheel once again. I actually improved my eating habits, took off some weight, and became more confident being up and out of the chair.

Writing Your Own Affirmations

The following tips will help you to write your own affirmations:

1. Remember that affirmations should be short phrases, using specific examples regarding the situation you are dealing with and the change you would like to implement.
2. Keep it positive! Affirm what you want, not what you don't want.
3. Keep it in the present tense; make your statement as if the future were now!
4. Restate your affirmations aloud each day.

Once I entered the competitive racing world, I also used this technique to help me develop not only my body for competition but my mind and spirit as well. During my Paralympic years, I had affirmations posted around my apartment on my refrigerator door, my bathroom mirror, and my kitchen cupboards. They helped me change my mindset, self-talk, and self-perception. For example, while I have good race endurance, I am not naturally a quick sprinter and my starts were slow. I needed to change that negative into a positive, and I formulated affirmations to reinforce that change:

"My hands are light and I am quick to accelerate!"
"I am explosive and fly like the wind!"
"I can do all things through
Christ who strengthens me!"
(Philippians 4:13)

These affirmations were a powerful part of my training, and I recited them in the morning before my training workouts as I'd see them posted around my apartment. I believe they helped me to become a stronger and more confident racer.

Using positive words also enables us to reframe negative situations, turning them into positive ones. When I am walking up a flight of steps, for example, each step takes a lot of effort. I will say the word "Attack!" to myself before each step. This gives me power and a sense that I can use the strength I have to conquer the difficulty. Other negatives of everyday living are overcome in the same way. When I go outside after a snowstorm and there is snow to push through, I say:

> *"I enjoy the workout that I am getting*
> *pushing through this snow!*
> *As I push through snow,*
> *I am getting stronger!"*

By phrasing my new mental outlook in positive terms, I turn what is actually a lot more work into a healthful benefit, knowing that I'm pushing myself and getting stronger, both of which are important life goals for me.

Whether we're aware of it or not, we are talking to ourselves almost continuously. According to the National Science Foundation, the average person thinks 1,000 thoughts per hour, while a deeper thinker processes 50,000 thoughts daily. "Probably 90% of us are driving down the road thinking negative things rather than positive," says Dr. John Ingram Walker, a clinical professor of psychiatry at the University of Texas Health Science Center. "It's so common now to think negatively because we hear all sorts of negative news on radio and TV and read it in the newspaper. We essentially have to train ourselves to think positively."

Because our words directly affect our reality, we need to keep them positive! If they are constantly peppered with repetitive negative thoughts such as "My situation will never change" or "I'm stuck in this job/neighborhood/family/relationship," we must consciously interrupt the cycle and retrain our minds to think in positive, action-oriented terms, focusing on the power we have to make choices that will lead to positive change. The following statements do just this: "I can improve my situation by..." or "I can choose to leave this destructive relationship" or "I can begin looking for new job opportunities today!"

When we change our negative self-talk into positive self-talk, our whole outlook and attitude is changed. Though life may be filled with uncertainty, change, and unpredictable events that are out of our control, one thing is certain: we are in control of our attitudes! A reading I have on my office wall by Charles Swindoll says this best:

The longer I live, the more I realize the impact of attitude on life. Attitude, to me, is more important than facts. It is more important that the past, than education, than money, than circumstances, than failures, than successes, than what other people think or say or do. It is more important than appearance, giftedness, or skill. It will make or break a company, a church...a home. The remarkable thing is, we have a choice every day regarding the attitude we will embrace for that day. We cannot change our past...we cannot change the fact that people will act in a certain way. We cannot change the inevitable. The only thing we can do is play on the one string we have, and that is our attitude...I am convinced that life is 10% what happens to me and 90% how I react to it. And so it is with you...we are in charge of our attitudes.

From Attitude to Action

Over the years I have memorized scripture, which has helped me to calm my fears and keep a positive attitude even in stressful situations. In 1997 I traveled to Warm Springs, Georgia, for the National Wheelchair Championships. As I was getting off the airplane in Atlanta at 10:30 p.m., the flight attendant informed me that my daily wheelchair had been left behind in Minneapolis when I changed planes. They gave me a complete clunker of a wheelchair that was actually set up so I couldn't push myself. Since I needed to let the athlete transport van know I had arrived, the airline staff had to push me out to the van where the other wheelchair athletes were already waiting. I was the last athlete to arrive, and we still had another hour's drive to the training camp in Warm Springs.

After checking in with them, I went back into the airport to get my luggage and racing chair. It was then that I discovered my racing chair had a huge crack in the back wheel frame. There was no way I could compete with that kind of damage. I sat in the claims office, waiting in line and subsequently filing a report on both my missing chair and my broken racing chair. As I sat there, Bible verses I'd memorized came flooding into my mind: "When I am afraid, I will trust in you. In God, whose word I praise, I will trust; I will not be afraid" (Psalms 56:3-4).

Certainly this wasn't a life or death situation, but these circumstances were beyond my control and such verses brought a calm to my heart. Well over an hour later, I finally got back to the shuttle. The other athletes were furious—not at me, but at the airlines. "They're so hard on our chairs! Can't they see what delicate bikes we ride?"

In the midst of their indignation on my behalf, they couldn't believe how calm I was and they all remarked on my attitude. The reason I could be calm was simple: in my mind, I was already jumping ahead, looking to see what blessing or adventure might be around the corner other than competing in the race I'd planned on. I remember thinking that this could actually be a fun meet to be a spectator at! Certainly the pressure would be off if I weren't going to compete.

The next day the airlines got my daily chair out to the training camp. Coincidentally, my wheelchair manufacturers, Eagle, were at this meet and just so happened to have the exact wheels for my racing chair. We made the switch and I was able to compete.

That day at the National Wheelchair Championships, I set national records in the 400, 800, 1500, and 5000 meter events for quad women and was named "Outstanding Female Athlete" at the meet. While those honors and achievements were certainly wonderful, what was most rewarding and life-changing was the realization that living with a positive attitude had actually given me joy, peace, and energy that equipped me to do my best. I hadn't allowed negative emotions to drain and frustrate me physically and emotionally.

Looking back, it was certainly possible that I would not have been able to compete—life doesn't always go as we had planned—yet we are in charge of our attitudes every day. Living with a positive attitude helps us deal with the abrupt, unforeseen, and unpredictable events that are simply a part of life. Such events become daily opportunities to open ourselves to growth and an understanding that even these untimely roadblocks are part of a bigger plan and purpose.

Gratitude: Opening Ourselves to God's Power

One of my favorite parts of the summer is working at camps for families affected by disability through Joni and Friends, the disability outreach of Joni Eareckson Tada dedicated to serving people with disabilities throughout the world. The camps bring me in as a part of the leadership team and I facilitate groups, lead workshops, and provide counseling. I also get to play hard! One summer at the Spruce Lake Family Retreat in Pennsylvania, I was sitting out on a porch leading "Teen Time" with about 10 high school kids with disabilities.

Chrissie raised the question, "Judy, when you're having a really hard day and life just isn't going your way, what do you do?" I responded by sharing with Chrissie that gratitude, giving thanks to God for everyday blessings that I might be tempted to overlook, is one of the best tools I've got. I shared how I often use this tool when I have difficulty sleeping at night. If I'm worried about something I thank God or praise Him by going through the alphabet. "I praise you God for you are Almighty! I praise you for the Beauty of the earth! I praise you God for your Compassion...Thank you for Delivering us from sin..."

Just about then, it hit me! "C'mon guys, let's just do this together...right now!" I cried. It was the coolest thing as we went around the circle, each person thanking and praising God for everyday miracles. It was a "God moment" I will never forget, watching as these kids learned how an "attitude of gratitude" can change our world as it changes our perspective, giving us power to overcome.

When we thank God, we open ourselves up to the power of God at work in our lives. For years when I was a social worker on the rehab unit and days were hectic, I kept a "Gratitude Journal." Every night I wrote down five things I was grateful for that day. Knowing I was going to be doing that at night opened my eyes during the day to watch for the goodness happening all around me. Perhaps it was a conversation with a friend, a good workout, a smooth discharge plan with a patient at work, or just the peace and comfort of putting my head down on the pillow at night. Things didn't have to be big or profound for me to be thankful for them, but my "Gratitude Journal" opened my eyes to the blessings that blanketed each day...to God's fingerprints all around me.

Joni Eareckson Tada describes how giving thanks brought her back from a suicidal despair after a diving accident took away the use of her arms and legs. A vibrant horsewoman and athlete, Joni believed life was over for her. One day she began to give thanks—at first for just the small things like the sunshine at her window or the bird that chirped so brightly on the tree outside. Gradually, she began to thank God for the bigger things—her wheelchair that gave her mobility, the friends who came to take her out. As she began to give thanks, her world was transformed and she found power to face life with courage and hope.

Through my work at MeritCare, I lead support groups for people affected by disability. We cover many topics on coping with life's challenges and how to keep a positive attitude. Deanna Bakken is one of our gals with cerebral palsy who uses a motorized wheelchair and communicates with labored speech. I'll never forget the day she hit us all right between the eyes. With her head held high and great confidence, she said, "It's our attitude and not our aptitude that determines our altitude!" Wow! Right on, girl!

When I fly, there's a routine process I go through at airports nationwide. Because people in wheelchairs are hand-checked and don't go through normal security, we are directed to the side for security screening. Recently when flying to Minneapolis, I headed over to the airport attendant who was helping to get my bags through the screeners. Because I've done this so many times, I wheeled forward and began taking my shoes off, knowing they needed to be checked. Another airport attendant came forward with this huge smile on his face and asked in a loud voice, "Are you livin' your dream today?"

His question caught me off-guard because it evidenced such an upbeat, positive attitude in the midst of this tiresome, mundane process. "Yes, I am living my dream today!" I replied. "Are you livin' your dream today, too?"

He said, "Yes, I'm livin' my dream today. I'm livin' it *every* day!"

I so appreciated that brief, delightful, positive jolt of energy and just plain love for life! It got me thinking: do I appreciate each day, do I value where I'm at, where I'm going, and the people I encounter along the way?

Norman Vincent Peale said, "When you cast out pessimism and gloominess and cultivate the attitude of optimism and enthusiasm, amazing results will be demonstrated in your life. Even if your ability, training, and experience are less than others', you can compensate for almost any lack by dynamic enthusiasm."

Positive thinking does not always change our circumstances, but it will always change us, as the journal entry below indicates:

January 11, 1997

Lord, thank you for the positive attitude you are giving me about winter and these stormy days. The wind chills are still 50-70 degrees below zero, many highways are still closed, and it will be a challenge to get around. Yet, I have a list of projects for storm days/weekends, and am so excited about what's up ahead. I have life and health and a warm home, great job, super family, and friends. Let me not be discouraged with winter! I will not be discouraged with winter!

Attitude and Health

In a study reported in the *Mayo Clinic Proceedings*, "People who expect misfortune and only see the darker side of life do not live as long as those with a more optimistic view." Results of a personality test taken by participants over 30 years ago were compared to subsequent mortality rates. People who rated high on optimism had a 50% lower risk of premature death than those who ranked as pessimists. Besides a lowered risk of early death, many other health benefits were found to be related to a positive attitude. As a result of the study, optimists reported:

- Fewer problems with work or other daily activities because of physical or emotional health
- Less pain and fewer limitations due to pain
- Less interference in social activities from physical or emotional problems
- Greater energy
- Feeling happier, calmer, and more peaceful

What About You?

Tune into what you're feeding your thoughts. What are you watching on TV? What kind of music are you listening to? What are you looking at on the Internet? Does it build you up? Is it positive? Read books that encourage a positive attitude. Put reminders on your walls or refrigerator doors. Put the words you read into action by meeting life with a positive attitude today!

Frank Outlaw says it this way: "Watch your thoughts, they become words. Watch your words, they become actions. Watch your actions, they become habits. Watch your habits, they become character. Watch your character, it becomes your destiny."

I simply couldn't agree more.

August 21, 1996, Paralympic Games, Atlanta

Lord, daily I'm so grateful for the opportunity to be here. Yesterday I took fourth in the 400 with a time of 1:23.57. The race went fairly smoothly, and I was ready to compete—I felt relaxed and pumped and gave it my all. Of course, every athlete who doesn't get a medal is a little disappointed, and yet I need to focus on the positives of this experience—which isn't hard. This is my first international experience, my first Paralympic experience. I've been racing competitively for only two years (often it takes several years of intensive training and national competitions before achieving qualifying standards to compete at the Paralympic level). I compete in the 800 meter on Friday...I am ready by Your grace. I am physically, mentally, and spiritually strong.

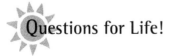

Questions for Life!

1. What kind of attitude do you try to embrace each day? What kind of attitude would your family/friends/co-workers say you have?
2. What are five things you are grateful for today?

Chapter 5

Make Each Day a Masterpiece

L ife can quickly be ended or drastically changed in just a split second of time. I see that truth played out every day in the hospital where I work and I know it from personal experience. How are you living today? How do you survive the crisis times that inevitably come? How can each of us manage the ups and downs of everyday living and make today a masterpiece using the keys we have in our hands right now?

We do it by breaking down our challenges, by setting boundaries, by clarifying our goals and priorities, and by giving our all— in short, by living intentionally every day that God gives us. When we use these tools, we move through challenges to joy and significance, living out our passions each day.

John Wooden was one of the most successful basketball coaches of all times. At UCLA his accomplishments included 10 NCAA Championships in 12 years with four undefeated seasons. John was given advice by his father when he was very young: "Make each day your masterpiece," his dad said. Wooden understood that we can't change the past, but we can learn from it. We shouldn't live in the future, even though what we do now can affect the future. We need to embrace life as it happens now!

Keys to "Masterpiece" Living

Over the years, I've come to realize that five simple keys can unlock the door to masterpiece living.

Key 1: Break It Down—Take It One Push at a Time!

One of the most challenging courses of my racing career was the Lilac Bloomsday Race in Spokane, Washington. This was a 12-kilometer race (just over six miles), which wasn't a long distance for me, but the challenges of this race were the steep hills, especially the dreaded "Doomsday Hill," which was a one-mile incline. When I participated in this race on May 4, 1999, there were 56,000 runners, walkers, and wheelers in the streets; the wheelchair athletes began the race about 10 minutes before the runners.

The day prior to the race, athletes had the option of touring the course by van, which helped us to develop our race strategy. For me, this was a time of mental preparation—they don't have hills like those in Fargo, North Dakota! As a wheelchair athlete with limited muscle strength, my plan was to traverse some of the hills, cutting back and forth as I pushed up the hill to reduce the angle and the steepness of the climb.

As I traversed the hills, I got off the push rim and was directly pushing on my spokes so that every ounce of my power was directed towards moving my chair forward. As I started climbing, I began counting, "One...two...three...!" My muscles were burning and my body was aching, but what a huge feeling of accomplishment when I got to the top of that hill!

I am thankful for Doomsday Hill. It reinforced to me that when we are going through painful crisis times or working on challenging projects, if we break them down into manageable pieces, we are ultimately led to the top of the hill.

Taking it "one day at a time" is a concept that recovering alcoholics know very well. Their 24-hour program is an approach to the challenge of staying sober. Recovering alcoholics don't swear off alcohol for life. They don't pledge to not take a drink tomorrow. They recognize that the biggest problem is to stay sober *now*. The 24 hours they are living at the moment is the only period of time they can control. Therefore, recovering alcoholics make a choice not to take a drink today.

Walking is a challenge for me every day. Here's how I break it down. When I enter the kitchen for meal preparation, I park my chair outside the door and I'm up on my feet, using the counters for balance. I do the same thing in the bathroom. When I get to the door of my bathroom, I lock my brakes, get up, and take the steps to cover the distance. Because I'm not strong enough to walk all the time, by exercising my legs in these ways I get the benefit of using my legs and standing tall. To strengthen myself for these everyday activities, I also use parallel bars for walking workouts every day. Because it is too boring and tedious to continue walking back and forth, I break it down into time sections that help me to accomplish a half-hour walk. I walk forward for five minutes; stand and do balancing exercises for five minutes; walk sideways for five minutes, and so on. Before I know it, the half hour is over!

If you have a major project, an overwhelming task, or even a mundane activity that must be accomplished, breaking it down into manageable pieces and doing a bit at a time makes progress possible and even enjoyable.

Key 2: Clarify Priorities

Identify the values that are important to you. Are you putting your energy into what counts? Intentionally direct your time, energy, thoughts, and money towards those things that matter the most, and recognize that sometimes those priorities change.

Sociologist Tony Campolo references a study in which 50 people over the age of 95 were surveyed regarding what they would they do differently if they could live their lives over again. Their answers to this open-ended question came back centered around three different areas. They would: 1) reflect more, 2) risk more, and 3) do more things that would live on after they were gone. This is a great question that helps us determine whether we are spending our time in ways that reflect our truest priorities.

Leaving the hospital after six months, with long leg braces and a walker, I was determined to make the most of the muscle strength I had regained after my accident. One year after the accident I went back to Craig Hospital to further assess whether walking was possible. Daily I met with the physical and occupational therapists, trying new techniques to maximize my mobility. Within a week it was clear that I probably did not have enough muscle return to walk functionally for my everyday activities.

I remember having a heart-to-heart talk with my dad, asking him why I should continue to work out and put walking as such a high priority. His response was, "Jude, we don't know what will come of the walking, but we do know how important it is for you to have as much strength as you can for the activities of daily living." That really changed my focus from walking to being fit. With this new emphasis, I discovered that the emotional and physical energy I'd been exerting with my walking could now be directed towards other new and exciting priorities in my life.

It was a longtime dream of mine to become a Bible camp counselor. I watched every year as Bible camp representatives came to Concordia and set up booths to interview potential counselors. In my heart, I wondered if this was something I should do given the new information I'd been given about my walking. How would a wheelchair manage in that environment? Would they be open to having a person in a wheelchair on staff, knowing it would mean more work for them?

During my junior year at Concordia in 1983, I took a risk and dared to share my dream with the director of Red Willow Bible Camp. To my surprise he said, "Judy, we'd love to have you!"

I took a step forward and dared to try. I knew I had a message to share with the kids, and willing people to help my dream come true. Was everything mapped out and perfectly planned? Absolutely not! Many of the logistics were unknown even as I agreed to join Red Willow Camp that summer. I knew I would be dependent on others at times and some things were going to be uncomfortable, including cold temperatures and rainy days. Because my body doesn't move much in the wheelchair, when I get a chill, it stays with me! Furthermore, there were questions in my mind about how the kids would relate to me. Would we connect?

Of course, the most obvious barrier was the camp environment itself. I knew I would require the help of others to:

- Carry me up the steps to the counselor's devotions and debriefing at the end of each day
- Lift me into the canoes
- Experience the "Mountain Dew Jump" into the lake
- Push my manual chair across stretches of land for the Wilderness Walk
- Take off the door of the bathroom stall so I could get in
- Install ramps on my cabin and around the camp

Clearly, I would stick out at camp and some things were just going to be uncomfortable. Was it enough to keep me away? No way! But sometimes hardship, embarrassment, uncertainty, or the fear of what others will think can keep us from stepping out.

Looking inward, focusing, and labeling ourselves by our fears and inabilities can paralyze us more than any physical condition ever can. The choice is ours.

That summer at Red Willow Bible Camp, my power chair got the workout of its life! With my physical and emotional energy redirected from walking to pursuing new dreams, I was able to be a fulltime camp counselor, leading twelve girls each week in Bible study and all the activities of camp. I didn't let the barriers or difficulties keep me from the joy of experiencing camp, nor did I let myself dwell on the very real hardships involved.

My work at the camp far surpassed my expectations both in terms of its impact on my life and on the lives of others. When I returned to school that fall, working out and being fit was once again a top priority and I plugged workouts into my daily schedule. The camp experience had served as a catalyst to get me back on track with my physical fitness.

I didn't fully realize the impact on others until years later when I met a young woman who had been one of my campers that summer. She had been so greatly impressed and intrigued by what I was able to do that she eventually became a physical therapist, dedicated to helping others achieve maximum mobility. Life's dreams all begin with making a choice, even when we don't know what the outcome will be for ourselves or those around us who are impacted by those choices.

Key 3: Create Work-Life Balance and Use Technology without It Using You!

Back in the 1980s, futurists predicted that by the turn of the century, Americans would be working less with greater leisure time, thanks to major advances in technology. They were wrong! Today, Americans are the hardest working and most productive nation in the world. According to the Bureau of Labor Statistics report released in 2003, more than 25 million Americans—20.5% of the total workforce—reported that they worked at least 49 hours a week in 1999. 11 million of those said they worked more than 59 hours per week!

Cell phones, laptops, beepers, fax machines, and email capabilities have blurred the boundaries between home and work, and we are bombarded with information every minute. Today, work can follow us into the grocery store or out on the golf course, cutting into our leisure time. While technology allows others to reach us anytime and anywhere and initially promised to give us freedom, we now live with the notion that every minute must be accounted for.

Many innovations that promised to make life more manageable have actually made the pace more frantic, and the more proficient we have become, the more responsibility we've taken on.

Today, it's not hard to pile many activities onto our plates. There are many opportunities for all ages, and often our free time has become as programmed as our work day. Anthony Gatto, a professional juggler and world record holder since 1989, has literally kept five clubs in the air for 45 minutes and two seconds. But when one or two more clubs are added, he can't juggle more than a minute!

We, too, often play multiple roles in our lives: for instance, I am a daughter, sister, friend, employee, and a volunteer with church and community groups. For me, balance is understanding my differing roles, not letting any one of them dominate at the expense of the others.

A recent survey commissioned by the Franklin Covey company reports that 83% of Americans desire to be better organized. I've discovered that the old-fashioned "to-do list" is a great tool to help me plan my days.

Each day I make a list of what I need to get done that day or week—the "must-do's." Also on the list are activities I will attend to if I have time—the "should-do's." As I complete tasks, I cross them off my list. Sometimes I carry those responsibilities over to other days if time does not allow me to get to them, and I feel great reward as I cross things off. Sometimes I write things down and cross them off after they have already been done just to let myself feel good about the accomplishment!

A healthy daily "to-do" list should contain elements of both professional and personal goals. In their book *Beyond Juggling: Rebalancing Your Busy Life*, Kathy Buckner, Brooke Derr, Dawn Carlson, and Kurt Sandholtz share helpful strategies used by busy professionals to maintain a healthy work/life balance:

- Alternate: alternators want to have it all, but not all at once! Their work/life balance is broken down into separate concentrated doses. They throw themselves into work with abandon and then pull back or quit altogether to focus intensely on their family or outside interests. Micro-alternators don't answer the phone during meal time, turn off the cell phone the minute they get home, refuse to check email at night or on weekends, and use all of their allotted vacation time each year. They consider their off-work time to be critical for deepening their relationships and for renewing their energy.

- Outsource: outsourcers want to have it all, but not do it all! They prioritize the activities in which they want to be personally involved and/or ways they wish to expend their energy, and then hire out the rest. Outsourcers achieve work-life balance by letting go of responsibilities, to free up time and energy for tasks they care about most. Outsourcers look to a reciprocal network of family, friends, neighbors, and other supporters who join together to help each other gain balance in their lives.

- Bundle: bundlers want to have it all by double-dipping! Bundlers involve themselves in fewer activities, but get more mileage by combining them. For example, say a group of women meets three mornings a week to work out, exercising while deepening friendships. The value of bundling isn't so much multi-tasking as multi-purposing. Its gift is in giving separate tasks greater meaning by putting them together.

⊙ Techflex: techflexors want to have it all at the touch of a button! Techflexors access technology to conduct their work almost anywhere at any time. Flexibility is crucial, as techflexors figure out how to maximize control over their days. In contrast to jugglers, techflexors don't use technology to increase their work hours. Rather, they use it to liberate those work hours from the rigid 9:00 to 5:00 structure. Techflexors can get up early, work several hours, and then take time off for errands, exercise, or spending time with the kids. Techflexors who work in an office use technology to enrich their personal lives, using cell phones or instant messaging to stay connected to family while at work.

⊙ Simplify: simplifiers *don't* want it all! Simplifiers have made a lasting commitment to reduce the time and energy given to non-essential activities, whether at home or at work. The payoff is greater freedom from stress, with fewer obligations to meet. Some people simplify from the beginning of their careers; others come to it after they've tried juggling for a while. In either case, a common characteristic is a willingness to make some sacrifices along the way, such as being willing to take a voluntary pay cut to work four days a week.

These tools have become strategies for purposeful living, helping me to become less stressed and more proficient in my daily life. For example, I "outsource" the mundane cleaning jobs around the apartment by bringing in a cleaning lady. While I can certainly clean toilets and sinks, I prefer to save my energy for other activities, and I perceive the help as a wise investment of my material resources that enables me to maximize my physical resources.

Having my dear friend, Susan Vitalis, drive me to speaking engagements is an example of "bundling." In addition to freeing me up to work on other projects, Susan provides feedback on my speaking engagement and assistance with my equipment. The drive is also a chance to deepen our friendship as we share our lives through conversation over the miles.

Key 4: Create Time Boundaries

"You need quiet like you need food and water, like you need sunshine and sleep," said Norman Vincent Peale. We all need time each day that is entirely our own. Ideally, this can be scheduled at the same time each day, allowing us to set it aside as regular mental, emotional, and spiritual refreshment. It might be 15 minutes after supper or in the morning before work or school. It is important to have a time of solitude that you practice on a daily basis. What you do during that time is entirely dependent upon what relaxes you. Take a walk, read a novel, journal, or simply reflect in the stillness of your own heart and mind. Allowing for that "time boundary" provides a margin for life—a blank space, uncluttered and open, that helps to define the "text" of our lives. Richard Swenson in *A Minute of Margin* says this:

Margin is like oxygen—everybody needs some. If we have too little, we suffer from the shortage. If we have too much, excess will not benefit us additionally. But having the right amount permits us to breathe freely. Margin is a space, specifically the space between our load and our limit. It is this space that enhances vitality and resilience. It is this space that guarantees sustainability. It is in this space that healing occurs, where our batteries are recharged, where our relationships are nourished, and where wisdom is found. Without margin, both rest and contemplation are but theoretical concepts, unaffordable and unrealistic.

One way to insert margin in your life is to take advantage of "down time." For example, when you find yourself waiting in line at the bank or the doctor's office, embrace that period of time as a gift! Increased periods of silence, with the television and radio off, allow the mind to relax and actually open up channels for communication. Growing up, our family would often watch *The Brady Bunch*. When we got a TV in the kitchen, we began watching it while at the dinner table at 6:00 p.m. Several weeks into this pattern, Dad decided it was better for the family to spend the supper hour more productively, so the television went off, opening the time up for us to communicate as a family.

Dad also established time boundaries for the family after my accident when I was in the intensive care unit (ICU). Because the family room in the ICU was small and often filled with others dealing with crisis situations, Dad felt that it was best that each family member have a two-hour break from the family room setting and get out of the hospital each day. This helped all of my family members to rejuvenate and regroup and return to the hospital refreshed and renewed.

Taking a day of rest each week is also a healthy time boundary. It is possible to be engaged in work seven days a week, but we need that one day for rest and relaxation. Go have fun with the family, goof off, do whatever lightens your heart—just don't work! The human body was not created to push seven days a week. If we want to keep our sanity and health, a day of rest is crucial.

Key 5: Give 100% Today!

John Wooden taught his basketball players that effort put out during practice determines the success of the team. "Give 100% every day," Wooden said. "Whatever you don't give, you can't make up for tomorrow. If you give only 75% today, you can't give 125% tomorrow to make up for it."

Giving 100% is about pursuing excellence every day and every moment, about living deliberately, consciously, and even intimately. It means being closely tied to the people, places, and things in our lives, and making the most of the priorities and opportunities we have been given. Today is a gift to live—we need to live it fully.

Giving 100% doesn't mean we exert all-out maximum effort every minute. That level of intensity would be an unhealthy recipe for burnout. Our cars are not built to race continuously, and so it is with the human body, mind, and spirit. Depending on the sport, even an athlete during a peak performance may not give 100% physical effort during the entire event. There is an optimal level of effort best for each leg of the race. For example, when I am performing my 1500 meter race, I am explosive off the start with 100% intensity, then I go into strong, measured power strokes for the majority of the race, finishing the final 200 meters with everything I've got.

But what about those ordinary days? The reality is, not every day of life is a high. In fact, the majority of life is made up of ordinary days. If we miss the value of ordinary days, we miss the value of most of life. Being fully present means we can embrace even the ordinary days by having gratitude for simple things, connecting with significant people, or making the day memorable by infusing it with special moments. Light candles, take a walk at sunset, use your "special" china, get out your photo albums and enjoy favorite memories. Today can be a masterpiece—the choice is up to you!

March 2, 1996

Lord, the last few days have been ordinary days, without a lot of enthusiasm in my heart. Forgive me as I've been giving less than my all. I've been lax to record eating, only giving about 90% in my workouts, eating some sweets. I thank you for ordinary days because without ordinary days we couldn't know mountaintop days. Thank you for your love that surrounds me on ordinary days. Keep me faithful to what you have called me to on ordinary days. Help me to live fully on ordinary days.

Having the opportunity to train for the Olympics was an undeniable high. Just about every morning I was wide awake at 5:00 a.m., anxious to start my day of training for the biggest competition in the world. What a huge adrenaline rush! Since then, I have come to realize that I can have that same eagerness and anticipation to live each one of my days as the incredible gift that it is. For the rest of our lives we will never get to do this day over again—are we fully present in it?

February 19, 1980, Craig Hospital

Today was a great day! My mental attitude made all the difference. I started my day with God and asked Him to help me serve Him however that may be, and I thank you, God, for helping me. You are terrific! Not a whole lot happened today, but everything I did, I did 100%.

February 23, 1980, Craig Hospital

I am shot today! It was my first day of independent living—no nurse, no aide, all on my own, and it's very tiring! Oh God, Mom and Dad will be here in one week and I'm thinking about being home again. I will be attending the Girl's District Basketball Tournament—last year I was one of the key players. I'm really going to miss doing that and it will be even harder watching it. Oh God, I wish I could talk to all those girls. I have so much I would like to say—that the game continues on, and we still have to give 100% every day.

For years, I kept the following quote from Elizabeth Elliot's book *Passion and Purity* on my refrigerator door: "Wherever you are, be all there. Live to the hilt every situation you believe to be the will of God."

I like that: be all there. Put yourself into life today. I don't always know what the will of God is for my life, but I know that this is where God has placed me today so I want to be all there. I want to live expectantly and joyfully; I want to embrace life as it unfolds and give my all to each new experience. I want to live fully the message in the following poem, "I Am."

I AM
By Helen Mallicoat

I was regretting the past
And fearing the future...
Suddenly my Lord was speaking:
"My name is I AM." He paused.
I waited. He continued,

"When you live in the past,
With its mistakes and regrets,
It is hard. I am not there.
My name is not I Was.

When you live in the future,
With its problems and fears,
It is hard. I am not there.
My name is not I Will Be.

When you live in this moment,
It is not hard.
I am here.
My name is I Am.

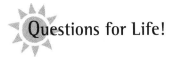

Questions for Life!

1. What in your life do you need to take "one push at a time"?
2. Do you have work-life balance? If yes, how do you achieve it? If no, how can you change your life to achieve it?

Chapter 6

Strengthen Your Mind

No doubt about it: knowledge is power! It breaks down barriers and gives hope, even as it uncovers options. But knowledge itself does not imply action, nor does it have the power to change our circumstances simply because we possess it. With knowledge comes the choice of what to do with it! An action is necessary to put into motion the wealth of possibilities opened to us through the gift of knowledge gained or given.

After my accident, my family and I were very dependent upon the doctors and nurses for information about spinal cord injuries, wheelchairs, and so on. Today there are more options available to the layperson, including vast amounts of information, research, and resources found at the touch of a finger on the Internet.

Most national organizations that are devoted to research, treatment, and assistance have informative Internet websites. Depending upon the issue, the following resources can also yield a wealth of information:

- County social service agencies
- Churches
- Community education programs
- Support groups
- Hospitals or health care centers
- Chambers of commerce
- Mental health agencies
- Yellow pages
- Local newspapers
- State or national organizations specific to your disease such as the American Heart Association, American Cancer Society, etc.
- Clergy
- Physicians
- Teachers
- Librarians

Get Pumped, Get Knowledge...Then Get Out There!

When I began my racing career, I realized that I needed to connect with other wheelers to learn the basics of the sport and to get the information necessary to take my racing to the next level. Initially, I connected with another quadriplegic from Fargo who had made his own personal racing chair with assistance from Larry, a local bike shop mechanic. As it happened, Larry would become a huge support to me in the future. Over the years, Larry and the bike shop, Island Park Cycles, did all the mechanical repair work and tune-ups on my racing chairs. Larry's knowledge, expertise, and enthusiasm encouraged me and helped me get out there in the racing world, making it possible for me to move forward into athletic participation again—fully equipped with the best bike possible!

I traveled to Minneapolis to learn the sport from some wheelers there. As I got more serious about racing, I ordered magazine articles from *Sports 'N Spokes*, acquired video tapes, and traveled to the University of Illinois several times to get materials to develop my training program and increase my knowledge of the sport. I knew my skills could best be developed by connecting with those who were doing the sport and doing it well. Their expertise, knowledge, and experience would empower me and help make it happen. I was doing my best to live the message in Robert Schuller's provocative quote: "Whatever you do, do it better tomorrow!"

But "getting out there" is not just about making our own dreams come true—it's also about using our gifts to serve and meet the needs of others. I first became aware of disability ministry outreach when I was in Romania in 1998 with Wheels for the World, the international wheelchair distribution program of Joni and Friends. Through Wheels for the World, used wheelchairs are collected in the U.S., refurbished in prisons nationwide, and distributed by teams of volunteers to people with disabilities in countries where the cost of a wheelchair often exceeds a year's salary.

As part of a twelve-member Wheels team, I remember those on the leadership team talking about how they provided support for people with disabilities in their home churches—they called it "disability ministry." I was puzzled—I had been in a chair for over 20 years and I'd never heard of such a concept. I'd also never realized the extent of the challenges many people with disabilities face, not only around the world, but right here in the United States as well.

Through Joni and Friends, I learned that most families affected by disability have little or no involvement with a faith community, that the divorce rate is exceptionally high, and that financial stress from medical expenses not covered by insurance is never-ending. Hearing this information, my heart was moved to return to my own church and ask what we could do to support those with disabilities in our own community.

I'm a member of a very large congregation, and my pastors were wholeheartedly supportive, encouraging me to bring together a team to develop a program that is now called Open Arms Ministry. Today, Open Arms Ministry meets the needs of people with disabilities in a variety of wonderful ways by:

- Providing one-to-one assistance in Sunday School classrooms to children with special needs
- Incorporating disability-friendly modifications to architectural plans for our new building that include pew cuts, power doors, accessible bathrooms, and lowered drinking fountains
- Providing weekly phone calls to homebound members of our congregation
- Devoting one week of our summer kids' camp to disability awareness
- Offering large-print bulletins and devotionals
- Assisting with Wheels for the World wheelchair drives
- Offering networking for counseling and financial resources
- Assisting with equipment needs such as wheelchairs, walkers, and other mobility aides
- Providing transportation

Knowledge is power that moves us forward to new possibilities, opens our eyes to see new horizons, and builds confidence. As a woman quadriplegic racer, I started at the back of the pack—I never thought I would be Olympic material! But as I continued to gain knowledge and put in time at the track, my performance improved and my vision expanded, leading me to two Paralympic experiences.

Similarly, when I went on my first Wheels trip I had no idea that five years later, with assistance from Open Arms Ministry and my employer, MeritCare Health System, I would set in motion the collection of over 500 wheelchairs, changing the lives of disabled people around the world. In both cases, getting information made all the difference in my thinking, my vision, and my actions. Information opens our eyes to what's possible!

Share Information and Empower Others!

In the same way we are strengthened as we gain knowledge, we can share knowledge to empower and equip others. In 1987 I was a graduate student intern in social work at the Sister Kenney Rehab Institute in Minneapolis. I remember dealing with a new 15-year-old quadriplegic. The very thing I represented—being in a wheelchair—was something he didn't want to deal with. Part of my role as a social worker was to get background information on him to find out what his interests were and what he was like before the accident. He would not say a word to me or even make eye contact. I went to my supervisor, Jim, who was also a quadriplegic in a power chair like mine. "What do I say to him?" I asked Jim. "How do I get him to talk to me?" I was so frustrated!

Jim said to me, "You give him information. Tell him how you live, how you went to college, how you drive a car, how you get around to perform the hundreds of tasks you accomplish every day. Knowledge is power!" I took that to heart, and in my next visit, I gave this young man information about my life. Bit by bit, barriers were broken down as I gave him vital tools to equip him for the life he would be living.

Years later as a social worker on the rehabilitation unit, a major part of my work was to provide patients and families with information about available resources to assist them to move on into life after hospitalization. Did they need home health services? Meals on Wheels? County social services assistance? Financial aid programs? Most of the time people were very open to working with me. They needed help and felt that I understood because I had been there. As we shared together, many times people would confide in me, "We trust you, Judy—because you've been there, you understand what we're dealing with."

During my summer as a Bible Camp counselor, I realized that I would need to share information about myself and be "up front" with my campers if we were ever to establish an easy comfort level with one another. Most obvious to the girls in my cabin was my bathroom arrangement. In the girls' bathroom we replaced a door on a stall with a shower curtain so I could get in the bathroom and still have some privacy. Inside the stall, I had a little table with my catheter supplies on it. (As a way to empty my bladder, I self-catheterize.)

The first night at camp, I would always tell my campers what had happened to me and how I used the supplies in the bathroom. "It sounds gross and it is kinda gross, but I can do it!" I would say. The girls would nod their heads, understanding and accepting that this was something I had to do. With the story out in the open and information given, they were just great—right there with me— supporting me in a situation that was new to them. Instead of making them uncomfortable, this honest sharing of information broke down barriers and walls immediately, setting the stage for honesty and openness right from the start.

Knowledge Brings New Direction!

I graduated from Concordia College in 1984 with a degree in speech communications/theater arts with the intention of getting my master's degree in speech pathology and becoming a hospital speech therapist. I completed one year of graduate school at Minnesota

State University-Moorhead and interned as a speech therapist at the Medical Rehabilitation Center in Grand Forks for the summer. During that time I was praying for a thesis topic—which never came—and I found myself deeply questioning whether this was truly what I wanted to do with my life. Speech therapy just didn't seem like the comfortable fit I was hoping it would be.

On my last day of internship I broke into tears as I finally admitted to myself that this was not the field I wanted to pursue. I had gotten my first car with hand controls that summer and I remember how I cried all the way from Grand Forks to my parents' cabin on Pelican Lake. "What am I going to do? This is what I've been working for! I've just spent a year preparing to become a speech therapist!"

As I discussed the dilemma with my parents, my mom suggested social work. "What does a social worker do?" I wondered. To find the answer, I connected with Mary Schroader, the social worker I'd had after my accident. Her wise counsel to pursue a master's degree in social work gave me the information and encouragement I needed to move forward. And little did I know at the time that the language training I'd received would prove to be invaluable in my career as a social worker on the rehab unit, where I would work with people with language difficulty following traumatic brain injury or stroke.

Sometimes along the road to our goal, detours can prepare us for what's ahead in ways we aren't aware of at the time. A relationship or connection is developed, a skill is learned, and patience is forged. When seen through the eyes of faith, even the rocky places are useful preparation towards the purpose God had for us all along. There is a bigger plan, and as we pursue knowledge and information—knocking on doors and seeking answers to our questions—our vision becomes clearer and His plan more attainable than we ever dreamed.

Coaching for Life

In her article, "Deepening Your Learning—Life Coaching," Linda David says, "To be both effective and fulfilled in our personal and professional lives today, we need to be learning continuously about ourselves, other people, and the many facets of our businesses and our careers."

We can continue to gain information and grow throughout life in many ways, but a very common key to unlocking that process can be found through Life Coaching. Just as athletic coaches are respected as voices of experience, life coaches work with clients in all areas, including business, career, finance, health, and relationships. Clients set goals and their coach works with them to meet and realize those goals. They form a partnership to develop the plan, implementing opportunities, strategies, and changes along the way.

In 1996 on a flight from Los Angeles to Minneapolis, I found myself seated next to a woman who first introduced me to the concept of life coaching. When she discovered I was training for the Paralympics, she suggested that finding such a coach to help me prepare for the mental game would be beneficial. A life coach herself, she took me through a session I found very helpful, so I followed her advice and worked with a life coach for six months, honing my mental game in preparation for the competition in Sydney, Australia. I spoke with my life coach twice a month for an hour on the phone. I brought the content of the conversation to the table and he suggested skills and techniques to move me towards my training goals. Even though I had a great support system going into this Paralympic training period, my life coach was someone I could talk exclusively with about the challenges of training at the elite international level.

Ann Gooding, a diplomat of the American Psychotherapy Association, says that life coaching is the fastest growing field, second only to management consultants, as people seek help and direction in order to lead more fulfilling lives. Coaches take a proactive role in examining clients' lifestyles and work styles in addition to their physical, emotional, and spiritual health. The International Coach Federation cites the following benefits of personal life coaching:

- Increased self-awareness
- Better goal setting
- A more balanced life
- Lowered stress levels
- Enhanced self-discovery
- Increased confidence
- Improved quality of life
- Enhanced communication skills
- Increased project completion
- Improved health and fitness
- Better relationships with co-workers
- Better family relationships

A recent story in the *Harvard Business Review* estimates the total number of life coaches at 10,000, noting the figure is expected to exceed 50,000 within five years.

To find more information on personal life coaching or to begin the process of finding a life coach who matches your personality and needs, contact *www.coachfederation.org* or *www.findacoach.com*.

Experience Personal Growth by Gathering Information

John Maxwell says, "You never change your life unless you change something you do daily." So...what have you learned and applied this month? When you get information, what do you do with it? What are you teaching others? What are you changing today? How are you growing?

It's important for us to keep stretching, learning, and applying new information. It's such knowledge that gives us the opportunity to grow and increases the potential in life, but only when we act upon it. When we make changes based on new information, we can simplify our lives, improve our relationships, lead a better quality of life, and experience deep satisfaction as we leave behind what wasn't working and apply the knowledge we've gained.

Recently I visited Sally, a 35-year-old new paraplegic who was just about to be transferred to a rehab facility closer to her hometown near Minneapolis. The hospital chaplain called to ask if I might visit with her. Sally had heard of me and wanted to learn a little about what the road ahead of her might look like.

When I arrived, she was in the room with her 10-year old son and they were just finishing their evening supper. Immediately we began sharing information about one another's experiences, and the questions and answers flew back and forth between us. She was so excited to learn the possibilities before her: "I'm so excited to begin rehab!" Her demeanor was bright and energetic, communicating that she was open and receptive to any and all information that would move her forward. I have no doubt in my mind that Sally will be successful and will navigate not only rehab but the new world before her with great energy and enthusiasm. As a resource-seeker, Sally's ability to gain and incorporate new information into her life experience will be critical to making her new life all that it can be.

Information Brings Healing

Chad Filley was eight years old when his mother entered the hospital to deliver a new baby. Raised in a small Midwestern town, Chad and his father had quite a drive to reach the hospital after the baby was born, so they stayed in a motel en route. The next morning, rather than heading for the hospital, Chad recalls his father coming into the motel room with a pastor, telling him that his mom had died giving birth to his new brother. Very little information was given to Chad about how and why his mother was gone, and he was left to fill in the blanks as best he could.

Third-hand information eventually filtered down to Chad, leaving him with the belief that his young, beautiful mother had died of complications due to negligence on the part of an emergency room nurse, who had slipped out of his mother's room to have a cigarette. As a result of this belief, deep anger followed Chad throughout his childhood: someone had killed his mother.

Years later, at the recommendation of his pastor and with written permission from his father, Chad and his fiancé, Candy, returned to the hospital where his mother had died to look through the medical records in a final attempt to resolve his anger and bitterness. In a deeply emotional meeting with the very nurse whom he believed to be his mother's murderer, Chad heard the truth for the first time. Everything possible had been done for his mother, whose internal bleeding had set in motion a fatal series of events that led to her death. Instead of being her murderer, the elderly nurse had been a constant comfort to Chad's mother, never leaving her side as she worsened through the night. In the final moments of her life, Chad's mother looked into the same eyes Chad looked into that day—eyes filled with tears and compassion, eyes full of comfort.

Seeking the truth and gathering information about his mother's death was an incredibly transforming experience for Chad, enabling him to let go of his anger and bitterness and move forward.

Knowledge is power!

While information is the key to empowering us to meet challenges, make changes, and live life fully, this only happens if we're ready and willing to act upon it. Resolve to become proactive with the knowledge you have, or the information you wish to discover. Unlock the door to resources that can take your game to the next level...and discover the power of living without limits!

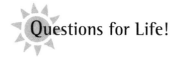 **Questions for Life!**

1. How are you going to strengthen your mind this week?
2. What is a passion of your heart that you can pursue today? What information do you need? Go for it!

Chapter 7

Set Goals

I t has always been my belief that if I have the ability to do something, I should do it! Around Christmas time of my senior year at Concordia, I realized I had the capacity to walk for my college graduation. Simultaneously, it dawned on me that if I was going to make it happen, I didn't have much time! If I was going to walk independently with my cane, up and down steps in my graduation sandals, each day from now until then counted towards making that goal a reality.

Over the days, weeks, and months that followed, I planned and prepared and practiced. For the first three years of college, I'd walked laps with a short leg brace on my left leg and a long-leg brace locked at the knee on my right. With each step, I would move the walker forward, take a step with my left leg, and swing the right hip forward. "Walker, step, swing leg, walker, step, swing leg..." over and over for 45 minutes to an hour. By the time I reached my senior year, even though I'd progressed to walking at parallel bars and using a cane, I knew walking without leg braces and a walker at graduation wouldn't happen unless I worked hard for it every day.

I went to the gym several times a day for sessions at the parallel bars or to walk short distances away from the bars with the cane. When I had a friend to spot me, I walked stairs and further distances in the halls of the auditorium. Mat exercises came next—stretching, push-ups, strength training, and crawling on my hands and knees for endurance. As I worked out that year, I visualized myself walking at graduation and my goal kept me focused and motivated!

It was good that I did practice because during one of my final workouts the week of graduation, I fell on the stage while practicing in those white graduation sandals. "Okay, I got that out of my system," I told myself. "Now I know what to do differently when the big moment comes!"

I did walk at my college graduation and at the Honors Convocation two days before, where I was selected as a student speaker and had the honor of leading the procession of faculty. Louise Nettleton, writing for the *Concordia Alumni News*, vividly recalls the drama of the moment:

Programs stopped fanning, children ceased stirring.
Everything was frozen in place except for the radiantly
smiling young woman making her purposeful way across
the stage. The applause began when she reached
President Paul Dovre. Her fellow Magna Cum Laude
classmates rose first, then wave on wave, the remaining
thousands that filled the room swelled to their feet.
Even those who had never heard of Judy Siegle were
aware they had witnessed something historic
and unforgettable. Those who knew her wept.

Goals set our lives in motion towards where we want to be, what we want to be doing, and who we want to be. A goal is simply a desire, something we have a vision of achieving in life. While many people want things, few are willing to work hard and consistently to get them. The difference between a goal and a dream is the act of doing! When you have got a goal, you are willing to take action to achieve it. Goals are the stimulus to discovering a wellspring of life. Some people just passively accept whatever life gives them. "Whatever happens, happens," they think. Instead, by using the tool of goal-setting, we can establish who we want to be and where we want to go, and map out a successful strategy to get there.

David G. Jensen, chief administrative officer of the Crump Institute of Biological Imaging for the UCLA School of Medicine, studied the results of those who have set goals against those who did not. His findings, as told in the book *Over the Top* by Zig Ziglar, indicate that people who set goals are healthier, wealthier, more enthusiastic, more satisfied with life and work, and have better relationships than those who do not set goals.

I have always been a goal setter. In high school, competition on the basketball court gave our team a vehicle to set goals for ourselves. Our basketball coach, Jody Weber, was notorious for making us run the lines in a drill we called "Ladykillers." It was a painful drill and we would do one after another. "This one's for Conference Champions!" she'd yell! "Now District Champions!" And, finally, "This is for Regional Champions!" By naming our goals, our coach put into our minds the very motivations and reasons we were training—the goals we were going hard after with each Ladykiller we ran.

February 17, 1977

We won! We are now officially the new Heart O' Lakes Girls 1977 Basketball Champions. I still don't believe it. We beat Perham in a very tough, close game. The final score was 42-49! Before the game we (the team) had a prayer and we said everything we would try to accomplish. We came out of the locker room so fired up! The gym was packed. Pelican got a student bus to go—the first student bus to ever get to a girls' game. The Madhatters (classmates who wore wild hats during our games) and all the fans were just great. At times the screaming was so loud my ears went numb. We played a beautiful ballgame—everybody. The whole game I repeated the words, "God, please be with us," to myself, while I played and while I sat on the bench, and I know He was with us. Although the game was really close til the end, we really kept our poise well. We never got shook really. We were so much a team—and most of all it was all of us who won the game. Janet scored 17 points and Lynn and I each had 9. After the game we were all crying and Miss Weber was so proud of us. We accomplished our first major goal—Conference Champions—and we did it out of the heart of our team, and we knew it.

Dreams Come True!

When I became involved in wheelchair racing, I wrote out many goals. Initially, it was learning the sport, getting the equipment I needed to participate, and then developing a training program.

I remember attending a race in Leesburg, Virginia, the year after I began racing competitively. It was a beautiful day and a fast track. That day I came within four seconds of a world record and was named

Outstanding Novice Athlete of the meet. The coaches were thrilled with my performance. From that moment on I began researching the qualifying times needed to make the Paralympic Team that would be competing in Atlanta in 1996, as well as the current national and world records in my events. I attended a racing clinic at the University of Illinois, where I received much of this information. I left the clinic with a long list of things to do—short-term and long-term goals—and I kept chipping away at my times.

May 13, 1996, U.S. Paralympic Trials, Atlanta, Georgia

Dear Jesus, how can I say thanks for the great experience in Atlanta? Yesterday I took 3rd in the 200-meter race and 1st in the 800. The 1st place is what I needed to get my spot on the U.S.A. Paralympic Team.

August 25, 1996, U.S. Paralympic Games, Atlanta, Georgia

It's hard to believe that this Paralympic experience—my first—is coming to an end. On Friday the 800 went well—but I got 4th place with a time of 2:44.35. It broke the old world record—but so did the top five places. Competition was just that tough. I felt boxed in and was a good part of the race. It was hard starting in lane 7 to get good positioning. And yet dear Lord, it went well. I didn't panic—I still got a new national record. Thank you Lord for helping me do my best. Help me to trust you with your timing and plans. Help me to be quiet these next days, to rest up as I start the next chapter in my life. The Paralympic experience has been such a terrific opportunity to be a part of.

Two years after the Atlanta Paralympics, I was competing at World Games in England in 1998. It was here that the vision of competing in the next Paralympic Games in Sydney, Australia, came so clearly into focus. All the athletes were staying at the University of Birmingham and we had only one small elevator for hundreds of wheelchair athletes! On the day of my first competition, I got separated from my racing chair and did not get to warm up on the track before the race. Warming up is critical for any athlete, but particularly for a wheelchair racer, who must prepare not only her body, mind, and spirit but her equipment as well.

A racing chair is set to run on a straight line. There is a steering mechanism, called a "compensator," that changes the angle of the front wheel. When coming into a turn on a track, you tip the compensator with your hand, changing the angle of the front wheel so that you don't have to steer throughout the turn. It is during the warm-up time that these critical steering settings are set. When my racing chair arrived just minutes before the race, it was too late to make these adjustments. I had no choice but to hop in and get set to go.

The race started and I came out strong heading into the first turn. I tipped my compensator—praying it was at the right angle—and the wheel turned too sharply, causing me to jump the inner guardrail of the track. I threw my weight back to get the front wheel out of the inner track before I was disqualified, but by this time I'd lost significant speed, leaving me behind the other racers.

I left the World Games with three fourth place finishes in my hand. More significant to me, however, was the goal that was birthed in my heart there in England: to prepare and equip myself for the next world competition—the Paralympic Games in Sydney, Australia, in October of 2000. To reach my goal of becoming one of the top three quad women racers in the world, I knew I had to be stronger and more prepared than I'd ever been before. Significant changes would be needed to reach that goal.

To medal at Paralympic levels, I knew I would need:

- Sponsors so I could compete in more events on a national and international level
- A reduced workload at the hospital so that I would not have to work fulltime and then train at the end of my day when I was already fatigued
- A coach to help me set a training program that would enable me to "peak" at the right time

While these goals seemed enormous and even somewhat unattainable, I put them in writing, posted them in my apartment, and read them aloud daily. As I spoke the words to myself, the vision became clearer and more manageable, and it fueled my determination to take each necessary step towards achieving my ultimate goal.

At World Games, I'd met track athletes who were affiliated with the Olympic Job Opportunity Program (OJOP), sponsored by the U.S. Olympic Committee (USOC) for athletes training at elite Olympic levels. Since American athletes are not financially supported by our government, many of us have jobs. The USOC encourages employers to become official Olympic sponsors and to allow training and competing to become part of a working athlete's job.

In a time of great competitiveness and demand in the health care industry, I did not think MeritCare would be able to support my Olympic dreams on a sponsorship level. Nevertheless, I met with Deb Soliah of the MeritCare Foundation to explain my goals. To my great astonishment, she expressed her desire to see MeritCare become my sole Olympic sponsor in cooperation with the OJOP program!

Immediately, I put MeritCare in contact with the USOC. There were eight slots for the Olympic Job Opportunity Program, and seven of them had been taken. To be eligible for this program, you had to be one of the top eight athletes in the world in your event, and I had achieved that with three 4th places in the World Competitions.

"Let's go for it!" the folks at MeritCare said, opening the door for me to work half-time as a social worker and the other half as an Olympic athlete and ambassador for a year before the Games in Sydney.

MeritCare also provided a sports trainer who served as my coach and helped develop my training program to take me to the next level of performance. I could scarcely believe that within months God had already provided all three of the goals I'd set for myself after World Games. I was on my way to Sydney!

Fine-Tune Your Game!

With every goal, there are necessary steps that prepare and strengthen you for that ultimate achievement. As Will Rogers once said, "Even if you are on the right track, you will get run over if you just sit there." Competitions locally, nationally, and internationally were steps to fine-tune and strengthen my game, assess the competition, and reach the highest level of performance possible.

The Para Pan Am Games in Mexico City offered me the opportunity to prepare myself again for international competition, off of American soil, where the track is different, the starting gun is different, and the whole living environment is foreign.

With every experience and opportunity to practice our skills, we grow in strength and in our ability to adapt and refine our performance. Embrace new opportunities to practice your skills; put yourself in new and different situations where changes might be called for. Even when things aren't familiar and you're out of your usual routine and environment, jump in and run! Your heightened ability to perform in new ways and at new levels, surrounded by new friends and faces, will bring a great sense of accomplishment and, best of all, joy in the process!

November 10, 1999, Para Pan Am Games, Mexico City

Thank you, Jesus, for this incredible experience. I am so grateful to be here. I took two golds and a silver. The silver was good for me, Lord, because it keeps me humble. I thought I could easily win the 1500 yesterday as I did with the 400 and 800. But I got behind and was never able to catch the Mexican girl. I will beat her at Nationals in the U.S. in July. I am still very proud of the three medals—knowing they are gifts from You, Lord. All that I am is from You...I have learned some good tips for future races as well. Help me to recall and implement them. I am motivated to keep training so that at the next international competition I am stronger and faster.

Connect with Other Goal-Setters!

Carole Inman, my triathlon partner, has completed 12 marathons. She is a strong believer in goal setting because goals serve to fuel and energize her life, propelling her forward. Instead of seeing goal setting as limiting, Carole says that her goals have opened her life to richness and a wellspring of life experiences she'd never dreamed possible.

Carole has experienced the ripple effect when even one goal is set and achieved, resulting in positive life changes far beyond her athletic pursuits. For example, setting a goal to run a marathon has changed the quality of her relationships, eating habits, and time management; she has met and made lasting friendships with many people in the running world; she has learned to be conscious about the fuel she takes into her body; she has learned to make good use of her time when significant amounts are required for training and putting in the miles. As a committed athlete and competitor, certainly Carole finds a thrill in meeting her goals. Yet, she describes herself as an average runner, finishing closer to the back of the pack than the front. But along the way, Carole also experiences great satisfaction in knowing that an extraordinary goal—running 26 miles—isn't limited to the elite athlete only. Ordinary people can reach extraordinary goals!

Kathi Tunheim, a friend and fellow Concordia graduate, began setting goals in high school on the advice of her speech coach and student council advisor. As they shared the value of goal setting and the positive outcomes that come from such a discipline, these mentors planted a lifelong seed in Kathi's mind.

She remembers well how her own goal at that time was to get to the state speech championship. Her speech coach encouraged Kathi to believe she could get there, even suggesting she could win. With hard work, practice, and determined focus, Kathi not only made it to the state speech tournament, she was named Minnesota's State Speech Champion three times in three different categories.

Kathi has been married to Bob for 19 years. Five years into their marriage they began writing goals together. Four times a year they sit down at Caribou Coffee to set goals mentally, socially, physically, spiritually, and financially. Kathi also meets with a group of four other women for goal setting, support, prayer, and friendship. They call themselves SOSSI—Sisters of Synergy Sharing Ideas. As part-time business owners, wives, mothers, and community volunteers, they meet every other month and talk about what's working and what's not, providing a safe place to discuss the challenges of finding a balance amidst life's many demands.

Shortly after learning about Kathi's SOSSI group, I attended a leadership conference in Fargo where I reconnected with some old acquaintances. As we each shared visions and goals for our own lives, we realized how valuable and joyful it would be if we started a SOSSI group of our own—to meet, to share, to trust, to encourage, to listen, to strengthen each other to reach for the dreams we hold in our hearts. As a result, SOSSI II has evolved!

Goal Setting: You Can Do It!

I lead a support group for people affected by disability and recently brought up the subject of goal setting during our group time. Most acknowledged the importance of setting goals, saying that doing so helps them to feel good about themselves, improves their lives, changes their environment, and gives them a great feeling of accomplishment.

Research reported in the *Journal of Counseling Psychology* in 2000 backs up these claims, showing that people with spinal cord injuries who are goal oriented are less likely to be depressed and more likely to gain acceptance of their disability than persons who are not goal oriented.

Realistically, however, the people in my support group identified obstacles to goal setting that plague us all:

- Limitations
- Laziness
- Procrastination
- Too many goals—overwhelming!
- Too many disappointments in life already
- Fear of success
- Fear of failure

Their responses are similar to most of ours. According to Zig Ziglar, only 3% of all Americans have a goals program from which they reap many benefits. In *Over the Top*, he identifies four reasons why the other 97% do not:

1. Fear: "the great inhibitor"
2. A poor self-image: can see the benefits for others, but believe "There's no way I could do that!"
3. A lack of fully understanding the benefits of setting goals
4. Not knowing how to develop a goal-setting program

According to John Maxwell, author of *The 21 Indispensable Qualities of a Leader*, "When it comes to commitment, there are really only four types of people:

- Cop-outs: people who have no goals and don't commit
- Holdouts: people who do not know if they can reach their goals so they're afraid to commit
- Dropouts: people who start toward a goal but quit when it gets tough
- All-outs: people who set goals, commit to them, and pay the price to reach them

Many people are resistant to setting goals. In corporate America, however, successful businesses have discovered that setting goals leads to greater productivity, both professionally and personally. TEC International, a worldwide support network for CEO's and business leaders, reports the following: "We can accomplish more and go farther if we dedicate ourselves to written goals, keep the goals on our corporate and personal radar screens, and follow through on the steps required to make them happen."

Angelo Kinicki, TEC speaker and co-author of the textbook *Organizational Behavior*, found that 68 out of 70 organizations examined in various studies enjoyed productivity gains as a result of management by objective. "Research on goal-setting shows that it is a very powerful technique to improve individual productivity and organizational effectiveness," he said.

Tips for Goal Setting

My friend Carole Inman and I have set New Years' goals together for the past eight years. After all, as John Maxwell said, "What you are going to be tomorrow, you are becoming today." We do this at the start of every new year and it is something we both look forward to. While statistics indicate most New Year's resolutions are given up within the first few months, Carole and I have continued successfully with our goal setting, helping each other to chart a course towards making our dreams a reality, supporting each other all along the way.

Here are the tips that have helped us set goals mentally, physically, socially, and spiritually:

1. **Start fresh!** Let go of past fears of failure related to goal setting.
2. **Dream big!** Don't limit yourself. The sky's the limit as to what you can accomplish when you set your mind to it.
3. **Write them down!** State your dreams as goals and develop a step-by-step plan toward reaching them! A goal not written is only a wish, and is easily forgotten.
4. **Be specific!** Set goals that are measurable, action-oriented, and timely.
5. **Be realistic!** Start with small, achievable steps beginning with where you are today. Set yourself up for success. If your goal is set too high, you become frustrated when you can't achieve it.

6. **Be flexible!** Some life circumstances may force you to make modifications to your plan. Some goals may need to be carried over from one year to the next.

7. **Be accountable!** Sharing with another person helps you to commit to the discipline. Find someone with a similar goal-setting approach. It's also fun to embark on the journey with someone else, giving and receiving unconditional love even when you don't reach your goals.

8. **Review regularly.** Keeping your goals at the forefront of your mind helps you stay on track yourself!

9. **Reward yourself!** Celebrate each success—even the small gains—to keep yourself motivated.

While goal-setting does require an element of discipline and may at times seem restrictive, it actually opens doors to new strength, growth, and endless possibilities! Whether you're training for the Olympics, preparing to walk a mile for a cause you believe in, or setting a goal unrelated in any way to athletic achievement, the Olympic Creed by Pierre de Coubertin can serve as inspiration: "The most important thing in the Olympic Games is not to win, but to take part, just as the most important thing in life is not the triumph, but the struggle. The essential thing is not to have conquered, but to have fought well."

I simply couldn't agree more.

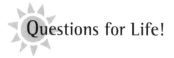

Questions for Life!

1. Are you a goal setter? If not, would you like to be one? What goals would you like to set for yourself?

2. What is the last goal you set for yourself?

My first family picture, Christmas 1960

Tim, Susan, and Judy—the family is complete

Go Vikings! My first year as a cheerleader, 1974

Family Fun at Pelican Lake,1968

Fun at the lake with Siegle cousins. From left to right: Mary, Ann, Susan, Tim, Judy. Front: Grandma Siegle, Steve, Grandpa Siegle

Uncle Ray and Aunt Ruth—my confirmation sponsors, 1976

Dad and I with the Solberg clan: back—Dad, Mike, Grandma Solberg, Grandpa Solberg, Dick, front—JoEllen, Katie, me, Julie

My high school Girls Basketball team, 1979. I'm #32.

My high school graduation, 1979

Friends celebrated my 19th birthday with me, three months after the accident—St. Luke's Hospital

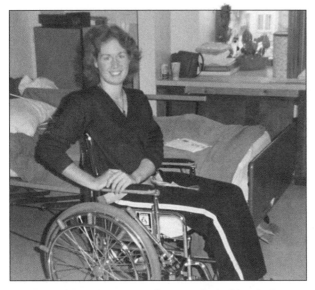

Ready and rarin' to go to therapy, Craig Hospital

Therapy with my #1 coach, Dad

My cousin, Ann, crowning me Concordia College Homecoming Queen, 1983

North Dakota's Outstanding Employed Disabled Citizen, 1990

Hangin' out with other quad racers after the Lilac Bloomsday Race,
Spokane, WA

Gearing up for fun on the slopes!

Competing in the Riverfront Days Triathlon with friend, Carole Inman

Cousin Julie and I celebrating a resounding victory at the annual
family shuffleboard tournament!

Jill Engelstad and me enjoying a traditional
worship service in Romania with Wheels for
the World

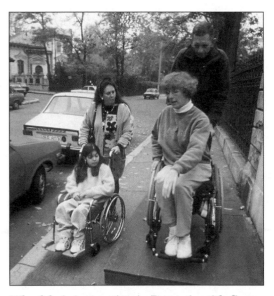

Wheelchair instruction in Romania with first
time wheelchair users

The Siegle family at my sendoff rally for Atlanta Paralympics

Competing in Atlanta Paralympics

World Games in England, Sister Susan, Brother Tim

Tim, Mom, Susan, and Dad—My fan club at the World Games

My new Olympic wardrobe in Sydney, Australia

Being introduced on the jumbotron in the Olympic Stadium

Fun at Olympic Stadium with friends, Joni Eareckson Tada and Jean Driscoll

Mom and Dad at Olympic Stadium

Facilitating a women's group at a Joni and Friends Family Retreat

Chapter 8

Create a Circle of Support

I believe we are created by God to be in relationship with others. We were never intended to travel this journey of life alone. We gain and grow from interaction with others, and we need others in order to be fully human, to laugh, to cry, to motivate, to be encouraged, and to be challenged.

There are different levels and circles of support: family, extended family, co-workers, neighbors, community groups, church contacts, medical communities, household supports, interest groups, support groups, and professional community supports, to name just a few. As we get to know others and establish a trusted, valued relationship, these people can become part of our circle of support. Sometimes this circle includes close friends; at other times trained professionals can be retained to ask the tough questions or to provide information and resources to motivate us to move forward. People come and go in these circles of support, and that ebb and flow is a natural part of life.

Sometimes we find ourselves alone, yet we still can be growing in positive ways, taking advantage of the peace and solitude to recharge and redirect our life plan. It can be during these "alone" times that we get to know ourselves better and learn to stand on our own two feet. Sometimes when we are alone we grow closer in our relationship with God, depending upon Him to give us strength beyond our own.

If you are going off to college, moving to a new city, taking a new job, or experiencing a major loss or transition in life, you may be experiencing these changes alone. Be aware of the circles of support you need, consciously developing them through all the differing stages of life.

In my support group for people with disabilities, I stress the need to be connected with others, even when it requires significant effort to "get out there." I tell my group members that even during the winter months, when it is easier to just stay inside and not be part of things, we need to do our best to get out there. We need other people! There's a give and take in life that is so important to our attitude and personal growth. We must strive to connect with people, even during those times when it seems easier to simply "cocoon" ourselves away.

Develop Relationships: It's Worth the Work!

Friendships Give Us Strength

Friends give us encouragement to "keep on keepin' on!" These are the people who see our abilities, even when we don't see them ourselves. Before my accident, I had been a maid at Fair Hills Resort on Pelican Lake in Minnesota. After the accident, the support of the people at Fair Hills was amazing! Dave and Barb Kaldahl, the owners and managers, arranged a benefit hootenanny and raised thousands of dollars to help with my expenses. The following spring, they told me they would have a job for me as a store clerk, answering the phone, taking registration, and doing light bookkeeping. They didn't even question whether or not I could do it.

Back then, in the early 1980s, buildings did not have to be wheelchair accessible, but Fair Hills put up ramps around the resort, allowing me to fit right in. They even let me set up my exercise bike in the store office. Dave would help me exercise my legs each day and would also go for walks with me around the pool area, increasing my strength and confidence. As for my office skills, back then I certainly wouldn't have won any records for my penmanship—I was writing with my left, non-dominant hand—but Dave had me paying the bills. We'd laugh, wondering how the postman ever delivered those bills! But since the checks were cashed, we assumed they got to where they were supposed to go. The people at Fair Hills were wonderful friends who, at a time of huge transition, helped me to keep going forward in life.

Friendships Expand Our World

It was through a call from my dear friend Jill Engelstad that I first learned about Wheels for the World. Jill had been a physical therapist on the rehab unit at MeritCare Hospital and we had become close friends. Jill was married and working in Wisconsin when she heard Joni Eareckson Tada on the radio talking about Wheels for the World. She called to tell me about the program, and Jill and I eventually traveled to Romania together in October of 1998. While there, I saw with my own eyes people with disabilities being carried in the arms of their friends and loved ones, wheeled in wheelbarrows, or carried on stretchers to get to the wheelchair distribution sites. Among the many, our team met two fathers who came for wheelchairs for their daughters; one daughter had not been out of bed for three years; the other had not been out of the hospital since her accident a year earlier.

This was a huge eye-opening experience and a tremendous opportunity for me to become involved. I was able to teach the caregivers of these first-time wheelchair users how to navigate up and down steps, curbs, and rough terrain—and believe me, everything in Romania is rough terrain!

As a result of that trip, I became a Chair Corps representative for the state of North Dakota, collecting wheelchairs in our region through wheelchair drives. These chairs are eventually shipped worldwide for distribution by Wheels for the World teams. As a public relations spokesperson for MeritCare, I have been part of three wheelchair drives and have helped to collect over 500 wheelchairs for people with disabilities around the world.

Friendships have expanded my world in other ways, too. Karoline Pierson, a friend from Concordia, opened my world to thrilling outdoor activities I'd never dreamed of participating in again. It was Karoline who told me about Wilderness Inquiry. A hospital administrator and a real go-get 'em kind of gal, she got us both excited about venturing to the Apostle Islands in Lake Superior to experience a kayaking trip. Together we survived the "Tip-and-Roll Test" that proved our ability to remain calm and get out of our kayak should it flip over in rough waters. On our trip, we explored sunken ships, paddled through caves, enjoyed campfires, and built relationships with others who shared a love of fitness and the outdoors. Thanks to Karoline, I realized that I could participate in adventures with minimal adaptation, and life's possibilities widened yet again. Without a doubt, her knowledge base impacted my world with thrilling results!

Friendships Communicate That We Are Not Alone

A Joni and Friends Family Retreat is one of the most profound examples of building a circle of support that I have ever experienced. Many times these families affected by disability feel they are all alone in a world that does not understand their challenges and the day-to-day difficulties they face. The heartfelt connection that occurs at Family Retreat and the support provided between these families who understand each others' reality brings the joy of acceptance and an unconditional support seldom seen in the "real world."

The Lafferty family attended their fifth Family Retreat in the summer of 2004. Their boys, Peter and Joey, were both diagnosed with Duchenne Muscular Dystrophy when they were one and a half and three and a half years old. This is a progressive muscle-wasting disease that affects all muscle groups. Their parents, Tim and Joan, have walked through steps of grief that included watching their sons lose their ability to walk, eventually moving from manual to power wheelchairs as they gradually became weaker.

The first two years the Laffertys attended Family Retreat as participants. Joan said it was an incredible experience to connect with other families to see how they were making it, to share the hardships of life with people who understood. She has found that each year when they return, new friendships are made and old ones are deepened as they share their struggles with one another. Throughout the year, they email or call other families from Retreat, knowing their support system is only a phone call away. For the past three years Joan and Tim have been in a leadership role at Retreat, leading small groups for men and women. This year Peter worked as a leader with the junior high kids, giving back to other families what they were given themselves through Family Retreat.

Tim and Joan say they find tremendous strength by helping others—it takes the focus off of their own challenges. It is a wonderful blessing for them to be on the "other end," cheering families on, just as others have cheered their family on throughout the years. Knowing we are not alone gives us strength for the journey. As the lovely quote by an unknown author says, "A friend hears the song in your heart and sings it back to you when you've forgotten it."

In my apartment building, a widow named Betty lives next door to me. She has a grown son in town, but lives alone. Several years ago we established that we would share the *Fargo Forum*, our town's daily newspaper. I get the paper and each morning I write across the top of it: "Betty, please read and return!" and place it outside my door. She reads it and returns it at the end of the day, sometimes with a piece of pie, a caramel roll, or some cookies. This system has worked great for years. Not too long ago, in my morning haste, it dawned on me that since we have this routine down now, I didn't think it was necessary to take the time to write the same message every single morning on the paper. So that morning I wrote out a different message: "Betty, the newspaper is here. Take it—I know you have it. I won't be writing notes anymore because I think we have this down! Have a good day!" This was fine with me—I wouldn't have to take the time every morning to write those notes!

Weeks passed and I was going to be leaving on vacation. I thought I'd better write a note for Betty so she wouldn't think something had happened to me. So, I wrote out, "Betty, tomorrow I leave for vacation. I know you have the newspapers. I get back on Sunday and I look forward to talking to you when I return. Have a great week." I got home at the end of the day and there was a note across the top of the paper from Betty: "Judy, it was wonderful to get your note. It was so good to hear from you! Have a wonderful vacation. I look forward to talking to you when you get home." My heart just sank because I had not been aware that these words mindlessly scrawled across the top of the paper each morning actually did mean something to Betty.

Giving and receiving positive human contact reinforces that we are not in this world alone. It can be as simple as your smile, your attitude, a small act of kindness, or a note of encouragement that can mean the world to someone and brighten their day. I have gone back to writing notes to Betty on the paper each morning. It means a lot to Betty, so it means a lot to me.

Friendships Help Us Reach Our Dreams

During the Paralympics, riding the bus in Olympic Village was an adventure in itself! Everyone riding the bus was decked out in Olympic gear, sporting their national colors. There were athletes with a variety of disabilities: wheelchair athletes, dwarf athletes, amputee athletes (who had the artificial arm or leg they used for competition sitting right there in their laps), and visually impaired athletes (accompanied by their white cane, their guide dog, or guide person).

I remember sitting next to a young man on a manual scooter. He had one full-size leg that he used to propel the scooter, a smaller leg he was sitting on, and two very small arms holding onto the handlebars. Around his neck he had his credentials, as we all did, saying what we did in the Games: "Athlete," "Coach," "Doctor," etc. His credentials said, "Athlete." I thought, "Way to go, but whatever is your sport?" Sometimes you asked, sometimes you didn't, but I think it was the social worker in me that wanted to know the story behind the person! This time I didn't ask, but I wish I had—he could have been a swimmer, a shooter, a table-tennis player. While I don't know what his sport was, I'm sure he was there, just as I was, as well as every other athlete who made it to this event, because of the supports he had along the way. None of us got there by ourselves. There were people all along the way who cared for us, cheered for us, and said, "Go for it! You can do it! Way to go!"

My Paralympic experiences would never have been possible without the people who provided encouragement to me to press on towards my goals. Back home I was often at the track by myself, but some afternoons Jean and Hans Pohl would meet me at the track, unlock the gate, and watch me train. Island Park Cycles did my wheelchair maintenance work, and Tom's Shoe Repair made the adaptations to my racing gloves. Friends timed me at the track, and a physical therapist I know who is a strong runner ran intervals with me so that I could absorb the feeling of racing against another.

Prior to the Paralympics in Atlanta, MeritCare, Concordia College, Noth Dakota Association for the Disabled, Fairhills Resort, State Bank and Trust of Fargo and representatives from the community of Pelican Rapids participated in a send-off rally for me. The t-shirts that were given to my family said it all: "WE LOVE YOU, JUDY!" These are just some of the ways that my community and friends supported me. I did not get to these world events alone!

August 9, 1996

Dear Lord, such gratitude fills my heart this day. The rally last night was wonderful! Between 300 and 400 people attended. I was so shocked and honored. Thank you so much for the tremendous outpouring of love I felt and have been experiencing these last weeks. People have been so fantastic to me. Keep me humble, Lord! I know that all I have comes from You.

One of the greatest joys of my life has been to give to others the gifts of friendship, encouragement, and tangible resources I received during my racing career.

I met Shane Kvalevog when he came to rehab after a car accident left him a quadriplegic at age 20. He had been an outstanding hockey player in high school and was now facing the prospect of living the rest of his life in a wheelchair. As a social worker on the rehab unit, I met with Shane to discuss his adjustment to the loss and his future goals and college plans, as well as other crucial aspects of this change in his life.

Shane married his longtime girlfriend, graduated from college, and got a wonderful job with Microsoft as a product manager. Knowing how important it was to keep up his strength, Shane squeezed workouts in between his responsibilities at work and the demands of being a dad to three little children.

In March of 2004, Shane made a commitment to step up his workouts and push himself to the next level of fitness. He discovered that the harder he pushed, the better he felt. A real go-getter, Shane would work out over lunch or would rise early to work out before work. He would also push his regular daily chair on rural roads, eventually working his way up to 10-12 miles a day. The athlete in him was coming to the surface again. Knowing that I had competed in wheelchair sports, Shane's desire to participate in athletics once again led him to contact me. We talked about where he could buy a used racing wheelchair—typically very expensive—and I connected him with racers in Minneapolis who would also be willing to help him get started.

A month later, Shane's employers at Microsoft contacted me, asking for my input in a grand surprise they were planning to help Shane launch into wheelchair sports: "Judy, we want to raise the money for Shane's new racing wheelchair!" They had questions regarding the wheelchair details, potential costs, and chair manufacturers, which I gladly provided. I was also able to connect them with another Paralympic wheelchair racer in the area for additional help in getting the exact wheelchair measurements for Shane's wheelchair.

His co-workers sponsored an Olympic-themed fund-raising drive where friends could give donations at the "Gold," "Silver," or "Bronze" level. In a surprise gathering at work, his friends and co-workers presented Shane with a check to cover not only the cost of a racing chair, but some additional racing expenses as well. Shane got measured and put in his order for a new racing chair with Eagle Sports Chairs and ordered specialized push gloves from Harness Designs.

Shortly after receiving his chair, Shane contacted me about moving his workouts indoors due to increasingly cold outdoor temperatures. Since I'm no longer racing due to a shoulder injury, I offered Shane my rollers—a type of treadmill for wheelchairs—that were gathering dust in my dad's garage.

Dad dropped off the rollers at Shane's home the next day. With his usual vigor and determination, Shane pushed on those rollers every day. That combined with a strenuous weight-training program had him race-ready in no time, and he went on to participate in his first race—a marathon, no less!—several months later in Las Vegas.

"Judy, I'm hooked!" Shane told me in a conversation shortly after the race. It was thrilling to sense his excitement, to remember my own joy of discovering I could once again participate in sports, and to realize that I had been instrumental in opening this world to someone else. "I have no idea what this will lead to," he said, "but it's great to be out there in competition again!"

I sent Shane training manuals and a few *Sports 'n Spokes* magazines so he could continue to develop his training program. With a goal of participating in the Boston Marathon and the Paralympics, Shane is working hard to achieve qualifying times for these prestigious events. I have no doubt he'll be there soon...and when the time comes, I'll be cheering him on!

The joy of passing on to Shane what I've learned is an incredible feeling. As we discuss training techniques, classification requirements, and his participation in strategic races around the country, my heart is bursting with joy that I'm able to help someone else realize the thrill of fulfilling their own dreams.

Friendships Give Us Health

A 1999 study by Thomas Glass and colleagues from the Harvard School of Public Health reports that as we grow older, connections with people may prove just as powerful as exercising. In

1997, researchers at the Carnegie Mellon University in Pittsburgh found that going out with friends can boost our spirits and defenses against disease. The study found that those with a wide circle of social relationships were better able to resist colds, and enjoyed 20% greater immune function than those who were less connected.

Researchers believe that social connections enable us to deal with the stresses that lower immunity. Bruce S. Rabin, M.D., Ph.D., study co-author and director of the Brain Behavior and Immunity Center at the University of Pittsburgh, states, "Immune cells have receptors that bind to stress hormones. When this occurs, the immune cells don't work as well."

Strong relationships with family or friends can also motivate us to take care of ourselves—to exercise, eat right, and get medical attention when needed. A MacArthur Foundation study on aging points out that strong social supports can promote longevity by:

- Encouraging prompt medical care
- Promoting healthy behaviors such as walking regularly or quitting smoking
- Allowing direct expressions of affection, which in turn might increase our immunity to disease
- Providing practical help when needed—assistance with household chores, transportation, etc.

Social networks increase our sense of belonging, sense of purpose, and self-worth, which promotes positive mental health. Just knowing that family and a wide circle of supports are available can reduce negative emotional and behavioral responses to stressful events or other life issues and can bring us great joy...which itself is the best medicine!

Get Connected!

There are many ways to get connected. Try some or all of the following:

- ☼ Call a friend you haven't talked to recently
- ☼ Write a letter to a cherished childhood pal
- ☼ Join an organization or club to make new friends with similar interests
- ☼ Join a cause
- ☼ Get together with people to work toward a goal you believe in
- ☼ Work out by joining a club or start a walking club
- ☼ Join a class through a local community college
- ☼ Get out with your pet; seek out a dog park and make conversation with those who stop by to pet your animal
- ☼ Go back to school to complete a degree
- ☼ Volunteer at hospitals, churches, civic groups, museums, or cultural events
- ☼ Nurture your spiritual life by linking with a faith community

It's never too late to build friendships! Creating and maintaining your circle of support not only keeps you happy, it can also keep you alive and growing throughout life!

Questions for Life!

1. Think of a friendship that has expanded your world or helped you to reach a dream. Drop a note or give a call to say thanks.
2. Do you need to get better connected with others for a happier, healthier you?

Chapter 9

Increase Your Energy

A s a teenager I was involved in many activities, but it was through the discipline of sports that I learned to train my body. The process of teamwork, the structure of workouts, the requirements of discipline, the benefits of coaching, the camaraderie of teammates, the setting of goals, the perseverance necessary to keep pressing on, and the thrill of a win were all key elements that prepared me for a game unlike any I had ever participated in.

Regardless of whether you are trying to lower your cholesterol, lose weight, regain strength, or train for the Olympics, these are the key ingredients required to make positive changes in your health, fitness level, and physical condition, in order to take your health to the next level.

Thankfully, the discipline of sports and the athletic mindset were not taken away from me in the accident. Instead, these established principles were some of my greatest assets in helping me to move forward as a quadriplegic. When "the game" was changed to life in a wheelchair, I approached it with the same training ethic I'd use for any tough competition.

Work with What You've Got

Whether you're in rehab or learning a new physical skill or sport, the starting point is to accept and work with the muscle strength and body you have today. While there is a time and a place to grieve what you no longer can do—or the body style and gifts you do not naturally possess—accept and embrace what you do have and what is working. If you don't learn to work with what you've got, you will never move forward and discover what is possible!

After the accident, I was aware that I no longer had hand function. In rehab, I needed to learn a new way to do even the simplest things. I learned to feed myself, blow dry my hair, and brush my teeth all with adaptive equipment. As a patient, I had to depend upon others to do those things for me initially, but the drive to do it myself and become stronger overcame the awkwardness and embarrassment of learning to do things in a new way.

My efforts in rehab paid off. Eventually, the function in my left hand came back and I worked to strengthen the muscle return that each finger was getting. Where I was once a right-handed person, now I was going to be a leftie. And one fully-functioning hand has made an incredible difference! With that one hand, I can feed myself, style my hair, apply my make-up and handle all the girl-stuff that I need and want to do. Being willing to try meant that eventually my transfers in and out of the wheelchair grew smoother, my penmanship legible, my dressing more rapid, my endurance greater, my walking stronger. With these gains, my self-confidence soared!

The same can be true when we start a program of physical fitness or learn a new sport. While we might initially feel weak and incapable, those who allow their weakness and the embarrassment of their inadequacy to keep them from trying will actually lose function, and their condition will deteriorate the longer they stay out of the game.

Simply speaking, often attitude limits us far beyond our actual physical limitations. Those who restrict themselves out of fear or embarrassment effectively reduce and restrict their world.

Living without limits says "I can...and I will try!" Begin today by accepting yourself and your body. Start small! Small steps will make great gains when combined together over time.

Get Your Eyes Off the Negative: Don't Focus on What You Can't Do

We waste so much energy comparing ourselves to others, or thinking about what we can't do! Our negative self-talk can keep us from doing what we know we should do to promote our health, and gives us permission to procrastinate or eliminate options.

Recently a dear friend of mine named Kim was asked to enjoy a game of tennis with a friend whose skill level on the court was much greater than hers. Kim declined numerous times, believing herself to be incapable of meeting her friend's level of play, allowing embarrassment and negative self-talk to keep her from enjoying a simple game of tennis.

Wondering why Kim kept refusing to play, her friend pressed the issue and convinced her to get out on the court. To Kim's surprise, they had a great game! Kim's tennis game was not as poor as she had thought—she even blasted a few shots down the line that blew her friend away! Kim discovered that not only was it great fun to play, but her own game began to improve simply by being willing to try. Now, Kim and her friend enjoy a game of tennis whenever they get together, energized by the friendly competition and the added dimension to their friendship.

When I first started wheelchair racing, I was certainly at the back of the pack. Although I hate to admit it, as the only quad woman racer in my early competitions, I often came in last. In spite of that, it was such a joy to be having the sports experience again that I did not dwell on the fact that I had less muscle strength than most of the other wheelers—I was using what I had and I felt strong. The positives more than outweighed the negatives!

Look Ahead...Better Days Are Coming If You Just Get Off the Couch!

It's easy to look back and recount the many times we've failed in the past, but living without limits means looking ahead! Strength, energy, new vigor for life, and increased joy and enjoyment are all available by just taking that first crucial step towards better physical health.

What is the first step? For some it may be to drink more water; for others it may be getting a buddy to walk with or joining a local health club. That first step will be different for each individual, depending on age, ability, and personal goals. Medical research—and our own common sense—has proven that a change in one aspect of our health trickles over into other areas, improving the whole. There is a beneficial ripple effect upon our minds and bodies when even the smallest change is made. So get off the couch...exciting, energized days are just ahead!

Be Proactive: Use Your Contacts and Connect with Others

Now that you're off the couch, where do you go? Whom do you call? Where do you begin on your journey to better health and well-being?

In 1992, even though I was active in quad rugby during part of the year, I was looking for a sport that I could participate in year-round to improve my strength and skills. Knowing very little about wheelchair sports, I was thrilled to learn about wheelchair racing—a sport that enabled me to meet my goal of year-round activity.

It all started with a personal connection. My mom, hearing about my interest in wheelchair racing, told me about some friends whose daughter, Mary Oothoudt, was participating in wheelchair races in Minneapolis. At birth, one of Mary's legs had not fully developed, but throughout high school she had participated in many sports using a prosthesis. More recently, she had begun competing in wheelchair racing with her sister-in-law, Tammy Oothoudt, who took a gold medal in the marathon in the 1988 Paralympics. When I ordered my first racing wheelchair, I immediately contacted Mary and Tammy to help get me rolling!

What About You?

First, ask yourself what kind of physical activity appeals to you. It doesn't have to be rigorous! The most recent data underscores the tremendous value of simply walking for exercise, citing it as the one common ingredient in the lives of people who had maintained significant weight loss over a period greater than five years. Regardless of how you choose to start, it is wise to consult with your physician before beginning a program of physical activity. Perhaps he or she can suggest appropriate guidelines for your present level of conditioning.

Once you've made the decision to get started, talk with friends, family, local health clubs, or churches to find exercise programs that fit your schedule and level of activity. Connect with the people in your life or ask them to connect you with others who can support you in your fitness goals. Pick the brains of friends and acquaintances who seem to enjoy a level of fitness that you admire—find out what is working for them and utilize their knowledge. Perhaps these "fitness buffs," or even good friends who enjoy a brisk daily walk, would be willing to let you join them, lending their expertise and experience to you just when you need it most! This can provide great support, encouragement, and accountability...and lots of fun as you connect and enjoy the positives of healthy living together.

Discover the Joy of Recreational Sports

If you're one of those people who tried sports back in high school and your experience was not the best, hang in here with me—don't turn the page yet! There are a variety of sports that are non-competitive, healthy outlets of recreation. Your willingness to be open to new experiences could lead you to a passion you never dreamed you could enjoy. Just take a look at the following individuals and you'll see what I mean:

- ☺ Meredith is a 41-year-old mother and writer who never considered herself the athletic type as a teen, much less as an adult. She would never think of pursuing "sports" in a competitive, organized fashion. Yet recently Meredith discovered the joys of kayaking, hiking, and camping—all of which get her blood pumping in the great outdoors and have led to her improved overall fitness and sense of well-being.

- ☺ Julie is a 35-year-old Californian who left a prestigious career as a physicist to become a chiropractor because of her love of people. 20 pounds overweight, she began swimming in her backyard pool, walking the hills behind her home, and taking leisurely bike rides after work. One year later and 27 pounds lighter, Julie is now competing in triathlons with a fit and trim body she barely recognizes as her own. How did she get from point A to point B? One small step at a time, one "I can do it!" discovery after another.

It's never too late to open up a new world. After the accident, I believed my days in the sports world were over and that I would assume the role of a spectator. When I learned about quad rugby and downhill skiing, a whole new world of travel, experiencing the world, meeting others, and the thrill of participation opened to me. Wheelchair racing expanded my world even more, as I participated in competitions around the world, meeting other elite athletes and connecting in ways that never would have been possible before the accident.

It was at the U.S. Olympic Training Center in San Diego, California, that I first met Pam McGonigle-Stevens, a visually impaired runner from Philadelphia. She was born with albinism—no pigment in her skin, hair, or eyes, and only limited eyesight. One of the fastest women in the world and a quadruple medal winner in four Paralympics, Pam runs tethered by a shoestring to her guide runner, who is, ideally, significantly faster than herself. The inspiration I've received from my friendship with Pam has been one of the many wonderful blessings in my sports career, and this clearly would not have been possible if I had simply chosen to sit on the sidelines, watching others participate in the thrill of competition.

The good news when venturing into a new sport is that the playing field is always level for beginners—everyone starts out as a novice. Do not allow feelings of inadequacy or fear to sideline you. Living without limits means doing more than you thought you could do. So what if you were never a varsity athlete in high school or college? There are so many incredibly exciting opportunities today to become active, involved, healthier, connected, and invigorated through sports and physical activity. Determine for yourself that you will not let past experiences dictate your future success. With a little creative time management and rearrangement of priorities, you could be walking with a group of friends in your own neighborhood by this time next month. Or, like Julie, you could find yourself on the triathlon circuit before you know it! The choice is yours.

Redefine Success: Discover Your Own Payback

After the accident, I realized that I wasn't going to be winning basketball games anymore. While I certainly understood that success was more than winning, I knew I was going to have to redefine how I could feel good again about my body and my fitness level.

At the beginning of rehab, success was sitting upright without getting dizzy. By the time I left rehab, success was walking off the plane when I came home, with assistance from my dad, braces, and a walker. In quad rugby, success was smashing and bashing into another wheelchair to prevent a goal. In canoeing, success was walking the portages (the stretches of land that separate two bodies of water) with my forearm crutches, often over rugged terrain—the workout of my life!

In racing, initially success was just being out on the track; it was hauling two chairs in and out of the car after a hard workout; it was learning to set my steering mechanism just right so I could stay in my lane; it was pulling on racing gloves in the freezing cold with one working hand. Once I began competing, success was improving my time, increasing my distance, being asked by a girlfriend to participate in a 10K race alongside able-bodied athletes. Success was checking out national and world records, and realizing that my times weren't that far off. Ultimately, success was discovering that I qualified for the Paralympic Games in Atlanta, and again four years later in Sydney.

What was the payback at each stage? A sense of accomplishment and pride that I was doing something positive with my body, pushing myself to get stronger, accomplishing more than I'd ever thought possible. The paybacks along the way kept me motivated, moving, and mastering the inevitable obstacles.

What's Your Definition of Success?

Redefining success means reframing your circumstances in a positive light, setting yourself up to win in scenarios that are achievable today. If my success had been measured by the place I finished in the race, I would often have been disappointed. Instead, I shifted my definition of success to working on my stroke technique to get better performance or stronger attacks on hill-climbing. When walking the portages, I could have asked the guides to carry me. Instead, because I had the ability to walk, I reframed the situation as a positive challenge, doing it myself and loving the thrill of the win!

For you, redefining success might mean having the energy to practice T-ball with your grandson or participating in a charity 5K walk in your community. It could even mean fulfilling a long-time desire to take a self-defense or a karate class. Why not? If you allow yourself to shed your self-consciousness, the sky's the limit!

Taking Care of the Basics

When we take care of the basics of our lives—getting proper nutrition, exercise, and sleep—we are stronger and better able to enjoy all the beauty of life, and better able to deal with the crisis times that can arise.

Nutrition

In my high school days I was actually 30 pounds heavier than I am today. After the accident I lost the weight, but gradually put it on again over the years with poor eating habits, using food as a way to cope through my college years and during graduate school. I knew it was not good for me to continue to gain weight, because the more weight I carried around, the harder it was for me to have energy and to mobilize myself. To add to the problem, I was self-conscious—I didn't want to be out of the chair so everyone could see how heavy I'd become. I had a power chair at that time and if it had not been for my daily workouts, I would have been a lot heavier.

When I finished graduate school, I realized I needed to make some changes in my eating habits. I took off those 30 pounds through affirmations, by recording my daily eating, and with the help of my sister and cousin, with whom I formed an accountability group. We put ourselves on a daily calorie limit and gave ourselves two cheats a week. If we exceeded our limits, we had to pay $5.00 to the others. I kept this in mind and hung in there. I was ready to make a permanent change in my life, health, and appearance.

Medical Statistics on Obesity/Diet

- 65% of Americans are either overweight or obese, according to the U.S. Centers for Disease Control and Prevention. "Overweight" is considered 10-30 pounds over a healthy weight, and "obese" is 30 pounds or more over that weight.
- Medical costs for an obese person are nearly 38% more than for someone of normal weight, or $732 more annually.
- Information from the American Cancer Society reports that if Americans ate a healthy, balanced diet that emphasized plant foods and helped maintain a healthful weight, as many as one-third of all cancer deaths in the U.S. could be prevented, specifically cancers of the gastrointestinal and respiratory tracts, as well as oral, ovarian, and cervical cancers.

As I got more active and began to participate in wheelchair sports, I became more serious about what I was feeding my body. In 1998 I sat next to a nutritionist on a flight and told her my plans for competition in the Paralympics in Sydney. She encouraged me to take a multi-vitamin and calcium supplement each day, as well as to make several changes to my diet that continue to stay with me today. The first was to have five to six small, highly nutritious meals a day to ensure a steady resupply of energy.

Research and follow-up studies show that the major benefits of eating six meals a day are:

- Increased energy
- Less hunger
- Reduced food cravings
- Controlled blood sugar levels and insulin production
- Reduced body fat storage
- Increased ability to maintain lean muscle mass

I have found that eating six small, healthy meals and snacks, usually two to three hours apart, has proven to be an effective way for me to keep my metabolism going strong, ensuring consistent energy levels throughout the day. Snacks between meals should contain 100-150 calories, and portion control is critical. When I eat regularly, I'm not famished at mealtimes and can control my eating more easily as a result.

The second major change the nutritionist advised relates to the importance of drinking water. Of the six primary classes of nutrients—proteins, carbohydrates, vitamins, minerals, fats, and water—water is the most critical for growth, muscle development, and health. Water is the most abundant compound in the human body, making up about 60% of one's adult weight. It is crucial for biochemical reactions to occur in the body and it is involved in energy production as well as joint lubrication and reproduction. There is no system in the human body that does not depend on water!

Unfortunately, nearly one-third of the U.S. population is slightly dehydrated. Even mild dehydration, having a 1-2% deficit of body weight caused by lack of fluids, can have a measurable effect on mental and physical performance, muscle growth, and even long-term health. Since muscles are nearly 70% water, a reduction of fluid will affect their function. When your goal is losing body fat, water can be your friend, as it helps to take the edge off hunger, helping you to eat less. When it comes to peak performance, whether at the office, at home, or in competition, hydration does make a difference!

Like many people, I had an initial resistance to drinking water. The more water I drank, the more trips to the bathroom I had to take. As a quadriplegic, this sapped my energy. However, when my coach told me how critical it was to my performance to be a "well-lubricated machine," I overcame my resistance to drinking water and began drinking the suggested amount.

Since then, several studies have discovered a direct correlation between fluid intake and the incidence of certain types of cancer. Researchers in Israel, Great Britain, and the United States have observed that the more fluids people drink, the lower their risk of kidney, bladder, prostate, testicular, ureter, colon, and breast cancer. In Seattle, Washington, a study found that women who drink more than five glasses of water per day had a 45% decreased risk of colon cancer versus those who consumed two or fewer glasses per day.

Exercise: Use It or Lose It!

Regular physical exercise brings multiple health benefits, with more being discovered every year. Yet, while most people can gain measurable health benefits from exercise, recent surveys confirm that most people are not nearly active enough. The American Heart Association attributes about 250,000 deaths per year in the United States—or 12% of total deaths—to a lack of consistent physical activity. Most recent studies suggest that 30 minutes of moderate activity five days a week or 20 minutes of rigorous activity at least three times a week is critical to sustaining good health.

The physical benefits of exercise include the following:

- Exercise strengthens the heart, reducing the risk of premature death due to heart disease and/or heart-related illness
- Exercise strengthens muscles
- Exercise increases flexibility
- Exercise strengthens bones

- Exercise reduces the risk of diabetes
- Exercise reduces the risk of high blood pressure; it can also reduce blood pressure in those with elevated readings
- Exercise reduces the risk of colon and breast cancer
- Exercise helps maintain healthy weight

The psychological benefits of exercise include the following:

- Exercise decreases stress by releasing endorphins and/or creating an outlet for tension and anxiety
- Exercise improves self-confidence and body image, resulting from positive physical changes
- Exercise enhances moods and makes most people feel good, mentally and physically
- Exercise alleviates depression
- Exercise enhances alertness, comprehension, and memory

In his article, "How to Remove Barriers to Exercise," Paul J. Wort lists common reasons adults are not physically active and suggests solutions to overcome them:

Lack of Time:
1. Identify available time slots in your schedule. Find at least three 30-minute time slots per week you can use for physical activity.
2. Sneak exercise into your day: take the stairs instead of the elevator, replace a donut during coffee-break with a brisk walk, walk to work, do housework at a fast pace.

Social Influence:
1. Discuss your interest in physical activity with your supports. Ask them to encourage your efforts.

2. Plan social activities that involve exercise: take a hike with friends, explore a national park, take a dance class, volunteer with Habitat for Humanity to build homes for the homeless.
3. Develop friendships with physically active people by joining a group such as an aerobics class.

Lack of Energy:

1. Choose a comfortable time of day to work out. If you're too stiff in the morning or are not a "morning person," work out later in the day when your muscles—and your brain—are warmed up and ready to go.
2. Give yourself a chance—physical activity will increase your energy level if you just give it a try!

Boredom:

1. Vary your routine. Walk one day, bicycle the next, take a different route.
2. Join an exercise group or class.
3. Make exercise fun: watch TV or read a magazine while on the treadmill, listen to music on the stationery bike, or chat with a friend.

Lack of Motivation:

1. Set a goal for fitness that has real meaning for you. The following list contains common motivators that spur us on to become physically active:
   - A milestone birthday or anniversary
   - A medical diagnosis that can be reversed through exercise (i.e., diabetes, high cholesterol, high blood pressure)
   - An upcoming class reunion or family portrait
   - An exciting upcoming travel opportunity

2. Invite a friend to be your partner. Exercising with someone else can make it more fun and will motivate you to
   continue. A little healthy competition can also be very
   motivating!
3. Expand your world through new experiences, new people,
   and new places.

Fear of Injury:

1. Learn appropriate warm-up and cool-down stretches and
   exercises.
2. Choose activities that fit your age, fitness level, skill level,
   and health status.
3. Forget the "No Pain, No Gain" slogan! While some sore-
   ness is normal when you begin, pain is not normal:
   listen to your body and check with your doctor if the
   pain persists.

Lack of Skill:

1. Choose activities that require no new skills, such as walking, jogging, or climbing stairs.
2. Choose something you like to do that fits your personality.
3. Exercise with friends who are at your skill level.
4. Take a class to develop new skills.

Lack of Resources:

1. Select activities that require minimal equipment such as
   walking, running, jumping rope, stretching, stair-climb-
   ing, and dancing.
2. Identify and utilize inexpensive, convenient resources like
   community education programs, park and recreation programs, and church-sponsored exercise programs.

Weather Conditions:

1. Develop a variety of regular activities that are available, regardless of weather: check the availability of indoor venues such as the mall or your local high school gym.
2. Put on an extra layer to prepare for the cold, and always have an extra water bottle handy in extreme heat!

Travel:

1. Stay in hotels with exercise facilities.
2. Put a jump-rope, light weights, or TheraBand in your suitcase.

Family Obligations:

1. Exercise with the kids—find ways to spend time together and still get exercise. Ride bikes, play tag, cross-country ski at the park, etc.
2. Hire a babysitter and consider the cost as an investment in your health.
3. Jump rope or do calisthenics while the kids are playing.
4. Buy inexpensive exercise videos from trained exercise professionals and exercise while the kids are napping or at school.
5. Join the YMCA or a gym that has babysitting services available for members.
6. Start a mom's or dad's exercise club in your neighborhood, alternating as the "Trainer of the Day!"

Retirement Years:

1. Look upon this time as an opportunity to become more active, rather than less: work in the garden, walk the dog, play with your grandchildren, join clubs and organizations you didn't have time to enjoy when you were working. This is *your* time—use it healthfully.
2. Become socially connected with other active seniors.

3. Volunteer in community programs that ensure your active participation.
4. Give time to a favorite cause or church that will keep you moving.

The Importance of Sleep

"Sleep is as important as physical activity and healthy eating to our overall health, safety, and performance," says Dr. Carl E. Hunt, director of the National Heart, Lung, and Blood Institute's National Center on Sleep Disorder's research. He adds, "Inadequate sleep not only makes us tired, but it can make it difficult to concentrate, to learn, and to control our impulses and emotions."

William Shakespeare's line that "Sleep knits the unraveled sleeve of care" may be true, but the facts are in: America is a sleep-deprived nation. A survey done by the National Sleep Foundation in 2001 found that 63% of Americans do not get enough sleep. One in five respondents admitted to being so sleepy during the day that it interfered with activities at least a few days a week. In addition, those who sleep fewer than six hours a night were found to not live as long as those who sleep seven hours or longer. Finally, according to the National Commission on Sleep Disorders, sleep deprivation costs $150 billion per year in higher stress and reduced workplace productivity.

When you lack sleep, your entire body performs at a compromised level, resulting in being less effective at work, in relationships, and in creativity. Benefits from sleep can include:

☺ Enhancing weight loss
☺ Lengthening life span
☺ Improving memory
☺ Boosting mood
☺ Keeping mentally sharp

- Enhancing heart health
- Strengthening the immune system
- Reducing visits to the doctor

The benefits of napping have been illustrated in the lives of many leading world figures, including Albert Einstein, Winston Churchill, Napoleon Bonaparte, Thomas Edison, John F. Kennedy, Ronald Reagan, and Bill Clinton. Said Winston Churchill,

"You must sleep sometime between lunch and dinner, and no halfway measures. Take off your clothes and get into bed. That's what I always do. Don't think you'll be doing less work because you sleep during the day. That's a foolish notion held by people who have no imaginations. You will be able to accomplish more. You get two days in one—well, at least one and a half."

I take a power nap when I can for 15-20 minutes because it picks me up, enabling me to be more effective for the rest of the day. As you begin to strategize your own unique approach to improving your health, you too will begin to enjoy increased energy, decreased stress, enhanced social connections, better health, and strength and vigor for life. Even when preexisting health concerns do not allow you to be as physically active as you would like, take heart! Just being out there and participating to the degree that you can will improve your mental outlook and increase your physical energy.

Let me challenge you to take a risk, to do more than you thought you could do, to try something

Tips for Healthy Sleep

- Sleep is as important as food and air. Most people require between seven to eight hours of uninterrupted sleep
- Keep regular hours
- Keep away from stimulants such as caffeine and loud music
- Avoid exercise near bedtime
- Don't go to bed hungry
- Maintain regular bedtime routines

new and different, and to enjoy the thrill of a new experience. You can enhance your energy and well-being by taking your health to the next level. Begin today by putting your health on your "Top Priority" list, taking care of the things that are within your power to change. When you use what you've got, you realize you've got more than you thought you had! Now that's living without limits!

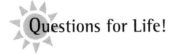

Questions for Life!

1. How are you taking care of the basics?
2. Is your health on your "Top Priority" list? Should it be?

Chapter 10

Embrace Humor!

I love humor! In fact, I love to laugh! Laughter brings people together, breaks the ice, calms fears, encourages trust, and builds a spirit of friendship. I find that humor is a bonding experience. In my childhood, my dad used humor in subtle ways, helping to bring our family closer. Dad left notes in poem form for us when we were out at night. We always checked in by signing the note, and the last one in would lock the door! Below are two samples of Dad's poetic humor:

> *Tim, Mark, Jude, Suze, Lynn, Carla:*
> *The tribe has grown, now don't ya see,*
> *What a major worry that makes for me?*
> *To feed and clothe and get the best,*
> *And in between to get some rest!*
> *The problem's the same as in the past,*
> *There are little jobs for those who are last!*
> *So turn out the lights and hit the hay,*
> *Lock the door so we can't run away!*
> *Also check your name on the back of the sheet,*
> *Or some of you might get locked out of their sleep!*

Suze and Jude:
Dance is over and we saw the crowd!
But you know what? We're oh-so-proud!
To know we've got kids that are like a queen,
And know that their ears and hands are always clean!
But we'll put away the crown and hang up the dress,
And hit the hay and get some rest!
Cuz tomorrow will be here, we'll never fear,
It's back to the routine and the place that's so dear!
Last one in gets all the lights, and to all a very happy
good night!

After the accident, our family was not laughing or looking at life in the same way. This was a new and traumatic experience we were going through together. The accident was a heavy thing, and yet as time went on we realized that we could not let it destroy what we had together or our family's love for life and laughter. We realized that we still had the most important things. We had life, we could be together, and we could be grateful for everything we did have, as opposed to focusing on what we didn't have and what had been lost. As we processed the changes the accident brought to all of us, we realized that life still held so many blessings, and we began to celebrate them once again. As we shared the new experiences and life's ups and downs together, joy returned to our lives.

Joy is an aspect of humor and can be found in the simplest of things. Sitting at the table to play Pinnocle with the family and using a card rack to hold my cards because my hand is paralyzed brought a smile back to our hearts. So did being lifted into a boat for a cruise around the lake, playing shuffleboard from a wheelchair, and going for "walks" with someone else providing the power behind me. As I relearned how to participate in the things that brought us all joy, laughter and good times returned. Simply celebrating small successes and embracing my re-entry to life brought joy, even though it was different than what we'd known before and felt a bit awkward at first.

In the midst of difficulty and tremendous loss, we can bring joy to our days by embracing activities, people, and places that we love. When we intentionally pursue joy, we engage in life, and humor will come. Life and relationships and the situations that come up can be funny...life is rarely perfect or the way we wish it was. The choice is ours...we can focus on what is wrong, or we can choose joy and laughter!

Here's an example: it was a snowy December night in my sophomore year at Concordia, and Mom was pushing me back to my dorm room. My right hand was in a cast because I'd had a tendon transfer to give me a pinch between my thumb and forefinger to allow that hand more function. My lap was loaded down with packages, and a birthday cake Mom had baked just for me was perched precariously on top of it all. With my birthday coming up the next week, Mom had carefully transported the cake from home for me to share with my dorm buddies. Somehow the front wheel of my wheelchair got stuck in the snow-packed sidewalk and the chair lunged forward, spilling the packages, the cake, and me along with them, out onto the wet, snowy sidewalk. In spite of feeling totally embarrassed, Mom started laughing and I joined in. Sure, it was a heartache that I was in that chair in the first place, but we had a choice to make—either laugh or cry—and we chose to laugh. Mishaps happen! Let's not take ourselves—and our goofy moments—so seriously that we can't have a good laugh at our own expense!

Humor Opens Up Opportunities

Victor Borge, humorist and writer, says that, "Humor is the short-est distance between two people." Humor is contagious and fun! We've all been in situations where laughter was coming from a group of people and we wished we were there with them, enjoying the connection that laughter creates.

Humor allows us to participate as it opens up opportunities. I traveled down to Winter Park, Colorado, one summer with my friend Jill. We met her boyfriend (now husband) Dave Engelstad there and set out to do some river rafting, alpine sledding, and tan-dem biking. I tandem-biked with Dave while Jill pedaled on a sepa-rate mountain bike. We strapped my feet to the pedals with a toe-clip and a rubber tubing and off we went.

The mountains of Colorado are just spectacular, and unlike my tandem biking experience in Fargo, we had some major mountains to climb. We were in a fast, high gear and our feet were pedaling very, very fast. My legs were pumping around and around and I was just hanging on for dear life while taking in the breathtaking scenery around me. We rode all morning, stopping only for lunch. Wanting to have the "total Colorado experience," we decided to eat outside on the deck of a charming mountain café.

As we wheeled into the town of Winter Park, Jill got off her bike first and came around to help Dave and me off ours. As they got my feet out of the pedals and I tried to stand, I realized that my legs would simply not bear weight. Instead of walking to the table with Dave and Jill as planned, my muscles were in such shock and trauma from the pumping workout they'd received all morning that my legs gave way! Who knew? We cracked up as Dave and Jill gave me a "fireman's carry" over to the table.

The funniest part of this crazy experience was the birthday party that was going on as we unceremoniously arrived at our table. Several elderly women dressed up in printed summer dresses and big hats were arriving with gifts. In the midst of their party, here were Dave and Jill helping me off the bike and carrying me to the table. Their eyes were just huge, wondering why this biker could ride a mountain bike but not walk. We had lunch, laughing so hard at what a hilarious picture we must have made!

While this incident could have been very embarrassing—and very discouraging as my body was not able to do what it was supposed to—having a sense of humor totally changed my perspective. Being able to laugh at myself allowed others to be able to laugh with me, enjoying our shared experience and allowing us all to participate, while opening up opportunities to see things in a different light. Being able to laugh at ourselves is so very important. Face it—we are funny!

Humor Releases Tension

In my first year of wheelchair racing, Channel 4 News, our local CBS affiliate, called and wanted to do a story on my racing. We set up a great day for the interview with their news truck and cameras out on the track, filming as I raced around it.

The TV cameramen wanted to get one last shot of me racing around a corner, off into the sunset. They set up at the start line and I headed out around the corner. At that point, I was still somewhat of a beginner and rather slow—wheeling was a lot of work! I went just a quarter way around the track and I thought, "I'm sure they got their shot," so I stopped and turned around to head back. To turn a racing chair, you pop it into a wheelie, completely reversing directions. So, I popped the wheelie, but with racing chairs being as tippy as they are and me not exactly an expert yet, I flipped straight over on my back. Strapped into the racing chair, I was just like a beetle on its back and couldn't get out.

The television camera guys came running out and flipped me upright. Caught unaware, we released the tension by laughing and were able to complete the interview in fine form, feeling a bit more like pals than we had before. I wasn't hurt, and it was a good laugh for all of us—not exactly the picture we were all after for the big "closing shot"! Of course, I made them promise they would not show me flipping over on national news!

A friend of mine, Care Tuk, is one of my life heroes and a hero of humor. When Care's mother was pregnant with her, she had taken a drug that was used to prevent miscarriages but was subsequently found to be dangerous. Care was born seven weeks prematurely and has had multiple health problems as a result. When I met Care in 1998, she was only 45 years old and already had survived 10 bouts of cancer and 62 surgeries. Five years later, she's had 11 rounds of cancer and 72 surgeries.

Care has dealt with her challenges beautifully and has become a very successful occupational therapist and a dedicated wife and mom. Along the way, she's used humor as her primary tool to cope. "Humor is coping," laughs Care. "There is no other option other than drugs! It's free, doesn't depend on insurance coverage, and requires no prescription—it's available to everyone!"

Care gets the laughter ball rolling with her collection of over 350 items representing the Disneyland character Goofy. She maintains a humor file, reads the comics, tapes favorite TV comedies, and believes firmly that joking makes reality more bearable. When we laugh, others feel more comfortable and accepting. Laughter levels the playing field. If we can accept our own situation with good humor and laughter, others will meet us halfway, on the common ground of our shared funny bones.

Laughter is sometimes the only way to get through our challenges. Care does get angry at times and will cry, but she always comes back to humor. Without humor, she is certain she would have gone mad with all the health challenges she has faced.

Humor Is an Attitude

Humor is an attitude, a choice to look at the lighter side of life and recognize that sometimes even the challenges can be good or funny. I've used humor in my interactions with people to add levity, break down barriers, and point out that there are some advantages to being a quadriplegic:

⊙ I have an excuse for my bad handwriting. Though naturally right-handed, I now write with my left hand because my right hand is still paralyzed. In the hospital setting where I work, this has become a standard joke, as I rib the doctors that I can read my own notes, but not theirs!

⊙ Being the first swimmer in Pelican Lake after the ice melted was a great way to taunt my "chicken" friends who shivered and shook while I swam gleefully about. Because I didn't feel the coldness of the water, I was often the first one in!

⊙ I possess the much-coveted handicapped parking plate. I joke that my portable plate and the great parking spots are the main reason my family and friends love to have me around!

⊙ Many people in our part of the country are bothered by mosquitoes. As a quad, I can no longer feel certain sensations from my shoulders down and, lucky for me, mosquito bites are one of them. Because my autonomic nervous system has been impaired, I don't sweat much either, so that smelly aroma that attracts mosquitoes in the first place doesn't follow me around like a cloud in hot weather. On the contrary, I'm cool and fresh as a daisy all year long!

⊙ Being a quad gives me a great reason to have a maid.

⊙ In a crowded, jam-packed arena, when you are a quad, you always have a place to sit.

Lighten up and look at the lighter side of life! Laugh at yourself...people love being around light-hearted people. Laughter and humor are contagious. A lighthearted approach to life does not mean being flippant or insensitive to the pain and hurt around us, but it does recognize that life is serious enough as it is; there is a time to cry, and a time to laugh.

Humor: Energy for Our Days and Health to Our Bodies

Dr. William Fry, a psychiatrist at Stanford University, was one of the first people to show the correlation between laughter and one's health. He says, "I believe humor is both a contributor to and a manifestation of our mental health. It reflects a positive orientation to life and a sense of well-being."

In an earlier chapter I discussed how medical research has proven that stress and negative emotions contribute to health problems such as heart disease and high blood pressure. Now, growing evidence suggests that the body responds to humor in the opposite way that it responds to stress. Laughter directly lowers blood levels of the stress hormones cortisol, epinephrine, and dopac. This often results in lowered blood pressure with less wear and tear on the heart. Other research shows that laughter helps the cardiovascular system by giving the heart and lungs an aerobic workout. In a study done at the Center for Preventive Cardiology at the University of Maryland, a good "hearty laugh" revealed good benefits for the heart. This study also showed that people with heart disease were 40% less likely to laugh in humorous situations than folks with healthy hearts.

In his 1979 best-seller *Anatomy of an Illness*, Norman Cousins reported the connection between feeling and healing. Cousins suffered from ankylosing spondylitis, a painful degenerative disease that can be fatal. He moved his hospital bed into a nearby hotel room and brought in classic comedy films featuring Laurel and Hardy and TV programs like *Candid Camera*. Laughing his way to health, Cousins' condition dramatically improved. In time, he no longer needed medications and was eventually completely cured of his disease. He ultimately left his position as an editor of the *Saturday Review* and joined the staff of the UCLA Medical School in Los Angeles to continue his mission in the scientific field of mind-body medicine called psychoneuro-immunology.

Arla's Story

At age 52, Arla was diagnosed with breast cancer. With a lifetime of choosing to wrench humor from even the most difficult experiences, Arla faced cancer and chemo determined to choose joy and laughter in every moment God gave her.

During the 45-minute drive to her chemo treatments in Santa Monica, California, Arla made a determined choice to turn what could be 45 minutes of agonizing dread into a full-fledged comedy hour. She purchased and stocked her car with comedy tapes, howling at the radio antics of deejay Roy D. Mercer as he spoofed radio listeners live on the air. By the time she arrived for her chemo treatment, she was literally crying with laughter, her body energized yet relaxed, her mind and heart light and lively.

In between chemo treatments, this same beautiful and flamboyant woman grabbed life by the horns, fulfilling a lifelong dream to learn to ride a Harley Davidson. Soon, motorists in her community began to recognize the smiling, blond, leather-clad gal with the streaming blond braids (attached to her two-inch re-grown hair) riding about town. People would approach her at the bank or grocery store, openly admiring her guts, her style, and her obvious zest for life. Glowing with laughter, few would have imagined Arla was in the midst of debilitating cancer treatment.

Four years later, Arla is still riding around town, healthy and vibrant, still smiling, and still spreading her infectious love for life. Cancer did not steal her laughter, diminish her beauty, or rob her joy. Instead, it only served to increase her passion for life and her determination to rejoice in the thrill of living, wherever her path may lead. And all along the way, the tears of laughter are still spilling over, cleansing, releasing, and bringing healing. "Laughter is God's special blessing for those who take him literally when He says in Proverbs, 'Laughter is medicine to the bones,'" she says. "Praise the Lord for extreme laughter!"

Guidelines to Appropriate Humor

- Always be respectful. What is funny to one person may not be funny to another. What is humorous in one culture may not be humorous in another.
- Never laugh at another's expense—unless they laugh first.
- When you are in a situation where one of the people is challenged, take your cues from the person in the more difficult situation as to whether you should laugh. Never laugh if they're not laughing. If you're the one in the difficult situation, remember: it's never too late to lighten up!
- Embrace humor and watch your energy, health, and joy increase while your tension and stress take a nose-dive.

Did You Know?

- It takes 72 muscles to frown and 14 to laugh—laughers often look younger than frowners.
- People who look at the bright side of things laugh more often and are healthier.
- Laughing is contagious—those who laugh and smile make others do it with them!
- Less than 20% of laughter is related to jokes.

- People are more likely to laugh in groups than alone.
- Males are leading producers of humor.
- Women laugh more than men.
- Most laughter occurs in general conversation.
- Speakers laugh more than their listeners.

Strengthen Your Funny Bone!

In his book *Never Act Your Age*, Dr. Dale Anderson gives the orders: fake it until you make it! Even "fake" laughter is beneficial, as it cues the cells into releasing endorphin-related chemicals. Mirror the behavior of lighthearted people—practice laughter and happiness. It truly is the best medicine! Here are some ways to get you started:

- Stand in front of the mirror each morning and belly-laugh for 15 seconds.
- Rent funny videos.
- Read the comics or humor section of magazines and newspapers.
- Build your own humor library of books, magazines, videos, and favorite TV shows.
- Remember humorous experiences and retell them to someone else.
- Look for humor and hilarity in commonplace, everyday situations—think Lucy and Ethel.

Questions for Life!

1. When was the last time you had a really hearty laugh? Find something to laugh about today.
2. Learn a joke today and share it with someone.

Chapter 11

Build a Spiritual Foundation

I grew up in a strong Christian home, where worshipping on Sundays, singing in the church choir, and attending Sunday school, youth group, and Bible camp were warm and wonderful parts of my life. From my earliest childhood, there was never a time when I didn't trust and believe that my heavenly Father loved me and watched over me with His tender care. On Monday through Friday at the breakfast table, Dad read from a daily devotional and the Bible, just as his dad had before him. This heritage of faith from my earthly dad only served to reinforce my childhood understanding of what that heavenly "dad" must be like—solid, dependable, loving, giving, tender, faithful, gracious, and slow to anger.

One Easter vacation while visiting Grandma and Grandpa Siegle in Montana, I took along a book to read that would ignite my heart to follow after Jesus Christ with a new kind of fervor. *Run Baby, Run* was written by a tough, drug-addicted, street fighting gang member named Nicky Cruz. It's the gritty story of his desperate search for God amidst the filth and degradation of New York's roughest streets. His eventual encounter with Jesus Christ radically changed Nicky's life, giving him the first taste of hope he'd ever had.

At 14, I couldn't have been more different from Nicky Cruz! I was a young, innocent, church-going teenage girl from the small town of Pelican Rapids, Minnesota, and yet I was gripped by Nicky's desperate search for God. As I read, I couldn't turn the pages fast enough, my heart resonating with the same passionate commitment to follow Jesus that Nicky had.

In high school several years later, I assumed everyone else felt the same way. Who wouldn't want to love God? I had so much to be thankful for. My diary entries from that time period illustrate how much of my life I shared with God.

February 9, 1978

Oh God, I've got so much on my mind so please listen. I guess you could say that our biggest worry is about tomorrow night—our game against Perham. If we win we tie for conference champions; if we lose we take second place. Oh God, I want us to play good so bad; it's such a thing of the mind you know—it's going to be the team with the best mental strength and it scares me. We've played some good games this year but we've also played some where we fell apart. God, I ask that you be our strength tomorrow night. Give us strength if we win or lose because if we have Your strength, well there's nothing better. Give us confidence, God, to play the kind of basketball we know how and keep us a team. Help us not to doubt ourselves and to never give up—even if they wax us. God, it scares me when I think how bad I want to win. Is that wrong?

We lost the game in double overtime and I fouled out. We had played our hearts out, yet this experience was an early lesson for me that God doesn't necessarily give us exactly what we ask for, or answer in the way we hope. This life lesson came at a critical time in my life and would help prepare me for a "change in the game" that was yet to come, where God's answer would be vastly different than what I prayed for, yet his strength would be sufficient for the challenge.

February 10, 1978

It was a hard one to lose. It means we tie for second in conference with Perham. The locker room was really upset at first but then we realized that we all did play an excellent game and we decided we were going to keep playing that good and meet them and beat them in districts. Oh God, help us not to look too far ahead, though, and I thank you for being with us that whole game.

Sharing my life with God and pouring out my concerns through prayer and journaling was a natural part of my life as a young high school girl. After my accident, I realized that my life, as I had known it, had come to a screeching halt. Very naturally, I leaned right back on the belief system I had established up to that point. Faced with a new and totally different reality, I would indeed learn to beat on His chest with my anger, clinging to my faith as never before. Most importantly, I would learn that faith tested and refined by the fiery trials of life is "pure gold."

In my freshman year at Concordia, I periodically wrestled with grief and questions. I remember thinking, "God, this is totally beyond me. I don't understand." I had no idea what my life was going to be like in a wheelchair. What kind of future did I have before me? I reached for my Bible to find words of comfort and guidance. When I came across Proverbs 3:5-6, it was a tremendous relief: "Trust in the Lord with all your heart and lean not on your own understanding; in all your ways acknowledge him, and he will make your paths straight."

"Leaning not on my own understanding" meant it was okay that I didn't have all the answers about why this had happened or what lay ahead. According to this scripture, all God was asking me to do was to simply acknowledge Him in the midst of my pain, and He would go with me through it victoriously. It was okay that I couldn't figure it out and probably never would.

During my sophomore year, a song by The Imperials meant a great deal to me. I especially appreciated the following lyrics:

"Praise the Lord, He can work with those who praise Him,
Praise the Lord, for our God inhabits praise!
For those chains that seem to bind us serve only to
*   remind us;*
That they drop powerless behind us when we
*   praise Him!"*

At that time, I didn't really know how I could serve God living in a wheelchair, but I could still praise Him even from the wheelchair. I drew encouragement and strength from the promise that He could still work with those who praise him, regardless of their circumstances. As I sang this song, I realized that this wheelchair that seemed to be an outward sign of limitation did not bind me and had no power to limit me or what God could do in my life. So, full of hope and expectation, I set my mind and heart to praise Him and opened my life for God to work His wonders.

The Four Corners of a Spiritual Foundation: Perspective, Power, Purpose, and Peace

Perspective

It's often been said, "Feed our faith, and our fears will starve." My pastor said this in a sermon once, and this anonymous quote appears in a daily calendar I have, too. My perspective both before and after the accident was that faith provides the assurance that regardless of what life brings—whatever fears we might face—we are not going through it alone. The assurance of God's presence is based on the truth in His word: "Nothing will be able to separate us from the love of God that is in Christ Jesus" (Romans 8:39) and "Even though I walk through the valley of the shadow of death, I will fear no evil, for You are with me" (Psalms 23:4).

Believing the promise of God's presence gives us comfort and a greater sense of boldness to step out into the unknown. We can take risks, daring to fall and fail, knowing that our heavenly Father is beside us to pick us up. Truly living without limits means we live in such a way that our fears do not rule us or dictate our course of action. Instead, we are motivated and energized by our faith.

Knowing that God is going with us is not a matter of faith alone. If we look closely, we can see His fingerprints all along the journey:

- When I finished graduate school in 1987 and got my first "real" job in Fargo, I moved into an apartment and lived alone for the first time. This was a big step! As Mom and Dad were carrying boxes into my new apartment, Dad hollered out, "I met your new neighbor!" In she came, and within minutes it became obvious that DeAnn was the perfect neighbor: we were both new to the community, both single, both Lutherans, both 27, and both pretty straight kids. We enjoyed the same things— movies, shopping, eating out—and DeAnn loved to host game nights at her house, which I loved to participate in. As if that weren't enough, DeAnn was always willing to help. Whether it was coming up with Halloween costumes or helping to clean up a broken bottle of V8 juice on my kitchen floor, she was literally God's hands and heart expressed to me for the 10 years we were next-door neighbors.

○ When Jill and I traveled to Romania with Wheels for the World, through a coincidental personal connection we were upgraded to first class on the flight and wined and dined all across the Atlantic—we felt like queens! One of my biggest concerns about overseas travel was whether the food would agree with me. Once we arrived, our group stayed at the Hotel Central, which was right next door to McDonalds. For me, this was heaven sent! McDonalds was literally a taste of home, and I knew I could eat there and never have to worry!

○ On our last day of wheelchair distribution in Romania, one wheelchair was left over. We wondered why no one had been given this nice chair. That day, I blew a tire on my own wheelchair and that "leftover" chair became my mobility, getting me around town and to the airport, making my final day so pleasurable. It dawned on our whole group that I was the reason that last chair was not given away: God was saving it for me!

When I look back to see His fingerprints in my life, I realize how intimately God is involved in the details of our days—smoothing our way, loving us in countless ways through circumstances, people, and events that we take for granted. When God goes with us, we are wrapped in love, joyfully anticipating what lies ahead on our journey.

God's presence with us also changes our perspective by broadening our viewpoint of our present reality, pain, or suffering. We tend to see the obstacles in life as thwarting our progress, whereas God may be using those very things to strengthen and change us for a bigger plan and purpose than our own. James 1:2 explains this beautifully: "Consider it pure joy my brothers whenever you face trials of many kinds, because you know the testing of your faith develops perseverance, perseverance must finish its work so that you may be mature and complete, not lacking anything."

A poem shared by Corrie Ten Boom further illustrates God's purpose displayed in our lives:

My life is but a weaving, between the Lord and me.
I cannot choose the colors He worketh steadily in me.
Oft times He weaves in sorrow, and I in foolish pride,
Forget He sees the top and I the underside.
Not til the loom is silent, and the shuttles cease to fly,
Shall God unroll the canvas and the reason why.
Dark threads are as needful in the weaver's hand,
As the threads of gold and silver, in the pattern
   He has planned.

—Anonymous

Power

My spiritual foundation gives me power to meet the challenges of my days. One of the most profound and powerful experiences of my life is what I call "the mile story," which shaped my life and viewpoint as much as any event ever has, next to the accident.

The last day of school during my freshman year at Concordia was a beautiful spring day. Everyone was packing up, saying goodbye for the summer. I went to the gym to do a quick workout with the long leg braces and walker that I used at that time. That spring I'd been praying for good workouts once summer came because I still wasn't sure what was going to come of the walking. So, that day I got my braces on and began to walk with my walker. My legs were striding out with just incredible ease! "I've been healed!" I thought. "This is it!"

I was flooded with thoughts: "Where do I go? Who do I tell? Should I call Mom and Dad?" As I was walking those laps with ease, I thought back to my days in Sunday School and Bible Camp and the scriptures and songs I had memorized. As I walked, I began to recite them back in my mind as a way to thank God. My healing had come!

At lap 11, I realized that perhaps I wasn't healed after all. My back was very tired and my hands were blistered and squishing from holding on so tightly to that walker. I didn't dare look at my hands and focus on the pain. Instead, I repeated over and over to myself, "I've got to make a mile!' Having been an athlete, I considered a mile—12 laps—to be a mark of excellence, so I pressed on. I came around that last lap so excited, thankful to God, and proud. I was just about to sit into my power chair when I lost my balance and fell backwards. Some of the teachers who were playing basketball in the gym came right over and helped me back into the chair. I couldn't believe it—I'd walked a mile! I was thrilled and went immediately to Campus Pastor Ernie Mancini's office, showed him my hands, and said, "Guess what?!" We called Mom and Dad together, overjoyed to share the news.

The next day I was anxious to see how my walking would go, but it was back to the slow, effortful walk. While it would have been great to be healed, I wasn't discouraged. My thoughts were so fixed on this power that had helped me to walk that mile. I knew I had experienced the power of the living God coming through in my life. There was no way I had the physical strength then to accomplish such a thing on my own. Even today, it would be a tremendous amount of work.

The next fall during my sophomore religion class, our professor gave the definition of a miracle as not just an astounding event, but one that reveals God in a special way. My jaw dropped to the floor. I realized that last day of school the spring before, God had indeed worked a miracle in my life.

I believed then, and still believe today, that God was saying two important things to me through that one-mile walk, with a fall just two steps to the end: first, "I'm with you all the way—you're not there yet, but I'm with you all the way!" I know the day will come when I will be whole, when I will run and jump and skip. Philippians 3:21 says, "The day will come when our lowly bodies will be transformed to be like His glorious body." What a day that will be!

Second, I believe God was saying that until that day comes, He will give me the power to meet the challenges of my days, whatever they may be. On that great and miraculous day in the Concordia gym, I experienced a miracle that has motivated and inspired me ever since. True to His word, since that time God has abundantly provided all that I have needed to face each day with strength and joy.

Purpose

I believe that if we have been given life, we have been given a purpose by our Creator. A critical cornerstone of a life of faith is the understanding that God has uniquely gifted and fashioned us for a marvelous purpose, using both our personal traits as well as our life experiences. With this knowledge comes tremendous assurance that our lives are not in vain, our experiences are not wasted, and our personhood is just as God intended. Even the rough places can be used to shape us on our way to fulfilling our ultimate purpose.

Rick Warren, best-selling author of *The Purpose-Driven Life*, says, "Only you can be you. God designed each of us so that there would be no duplication in the world." No one has your strengths, your weaknesses, your circle of influence, or your life experiences.

But how do we fashion an understanding of our life's purpose from these components? Perhaps answering the following questions will uncover the unique passion and gifting God has placed within you:

1. I am in my element when _____.
2. I feel most alive when _____.
3. The following circumstances or relationships bring out the best in me: _____.
4. _____ brings me joy.
5. _____ gives me energy.
6. I am passionate about _____.
7. My strengths/gifts are _____.

Identifying strengths is a critical first step to defining our purpose. A useful tool I have discovered is a dynamic new book called *Now, Discover Your Strengths* by Donald Clifton, chair of the Gallop International Research and Education Center, and Gallop Senior Vice President Marcus Buckingham. This exciting work enables readers to identify and translate their dominant strengths into personal and career success. Augmenting those strengths with determination, education, energy, and training puts us on a path to discovering our meaning and purpose.

Sometimes, however, we can get side-tracked by a determined effort to put energy into propping up our weaknesses. This yields, at best, a strengthened weakness—never a true giftedness. When we direct our energy and passion into our recognized strengths and areas of giftedness, we have productivity, satisfaction, happiness, and true brilliance.

For years I felt part of my purpose was to develop my walking to the best it could be. I gave it my all—no giving up for me! When I was training for the Paralympics, I realized my walking was getting weaker because my workouts at the track took all my time and energy. Weight lifting sessions were devoted to developing other muscle groups, leaving me less energy to walk into movie theaters or restaurants with friends.

Since my body had only so much energy, racing gradually took precedence over walking as I shifted my time, energy, and resources into strengthening a recognized ability rather than exercising a recognized weakness. I was aware of the shift, and though I still made myself get out of the chair, I recognized that I had the opportunity of a lifetime before me—world-class racing competition. Attuned to thrilling new possibilities, I realized that walking was no longer the ultimate end. My purpose had shifted to reflect my ability rather than my disability.

God has used this same principle to direct me in other areas of my life, revealing new purpose through recognizing and assessing the natural strengths He has given me:

- I am a "people person"
- I have personal experience in the medical setting
- I love the team approach, working with nurses, therapists, and doctors
- I am an optimist—the glass is always half-full
- I love a challenge

- ○ I am organized
- ○ I love juggling and prioritizing
- ○ I am a natural encourager
- ○ I thrive on discipline

My first job as a psychiatric social worker required all of the above! The very characteristics God had developed in me through childhood—and even those resulting from my accident and rehab—became a perfect fit for the medical setting.

While I was working on the psychiatric unit, a group of staff was gathering to develop a support group for patients on the rehab unit. They asked for my input and eventually I led the support group myself. It was rewarding and exciting as I realized God was using my story to greatly impact families and patients who were dealing with exactly what I'd experienced 10 years earlier.

My purpose was becoming clearer. When MeritCare expanded its rehab program to add another social worker, it was a natural fit for me, as I worked with trauma patients who had experienced spinal cord injury and other life-changing injuries like mine. It was meaningful, rewarding, and challenging. Best of all, it fit like a perfectly designed glove.

Around this time, I discovered that if you are a "people person" with a disability and are comfortable speaking in front of others, you get asked to share your story a lot. People knew I had sustained a huge life change, had moved on to live life fully, was training to become an elite athlete...and they wanted to hear the story!

On evenings and weekends I began traveling throughout my local region, sharing my story with service clubs, church groups, business leaders, and women's groups. During the Paralympics, when MeritCare allowed me a flexible working/speaking/training schedule, my speaking engagements increased, which eventually led to my present position as a full-time community relations specialist.

In my current position, I share my story as a motivational speaker nationwide, provide education and consultation to professional groups on disability issues, and counsel persons affected by disability. I also represent MeritCare through my associations with disability and relief organizations that have taken me around the world.

Looking back, it is clear: God uniquely fashioned me throughout my lifetime for this very purpose—no experience was wasted in His plan, no detour uncharted. The same is true for everyone. Discovering one's purpose develops over time. Natural abilities, inclinations, experiences, likes and dislikes, and even our difficulties are critical components in the hand of God as He fulfills His ultimate plan and purpose for us.

Peace

Faith brings peace of mind that God does have a plan for our lives. It was my freshman year at Concordia, and I was working out in the gym with my long leg braces and walker. On this day, my thoughts were running something like this: "Come on, Jude, how can there be a loving God? Look at all the pain and suffering in this world! Your own progress is coming so slowly!" I was angry. After my accident I had wrestled with questions that cut to the core of my heart. "Did I not have enough faith to be healed? Didn't God hear my prayers?"

That day, I remember just wanting God to touch my shoulder as I walked. I walked three laps—a quarter of a mile—and packed my things up. I went back to my dorm room, closed the door, and began to cry. Life was hard and full of unanswered questions. The telephone rang. It was one of the instructors at Concordia asking if I was planning to attend that evening's program where Cheryl Prewitt, Miss America 1980, was the featured speaker. I hadn't planned to go, but since he promised to save me a ticket, I decided to clean up, rid myself of the "poor me" attitude, and go.

That night, Cheryl gave a beautiful testimony in song and word about the power of God to heal, which she had experienced in her own life after a devastating car accident in her teens. She encouraged us to believe and know His healing power for ourselves. I sat in my power chair and knew I needed to talk to her.

At the conclusion of the program I worked my power chair up through the audience until I saw her face to face. "You say if we have faith we can be healed," I said. "I have the faith, even though I struggle sometimes. Here I am in this wheelchair—how do I know what God wants for my life? How do I know what He's doing in me?" I shared with her how angry and frustrated I'd been just hours before.

Cheryl listened with great understanding and compassion as I poured my heart out. Her reply was simple: the only way I would know what God wanted to do with my life was to get into His word and find out. She got out her Bible, wrote out some passages, and I went home and underlined them in my own Bible, studying them for myself.

That day I saw in His word that He did have a plan and a purpose for this world and a plan and a purpose for my life—even though it might be very different from what I'd planned or expected. I came across Jeremiah 29:11 (LB): "For I know the plans I have for you," says the Lord. "They are plans for good and not for evil, to give you a future and a hope." It was the beginning of a new understanding that my peace would come from the knowledge that the promises in His word were true, and that God's plans for my life were on course.

A Spiritual Foundation Births Hope

My faith in God gives me hope. During my senior year at Concordia, I was chosen to speak at the Baccalaureate service in my hometown of Pelican Rapids. I thought, "What on earth am I going to say?" Once again I went to Ernie Mancini for help. "How do I tell these kids what I've experienced?" I wondered out loud.

"What do you want them to know?" he asked.

"I want them to dream big dreams and pray big prayers!" I immediately replied. "I don't want them to put any limitations on what they can do and be!"

Ernie simply replied, "Then tell them that."

"Dream big dreams and pray big prayers!" I never would have imagined that would be my message. I was just graduating from college—I didn't yet have a successful career, I hadn't experienced traveling the world in athletic competition, nor had I delivered wheelchairs to third world countries. Yet, because of the accident, I had already learned that with God we can come through things we never thought possible.

In a strange way, the accident opened my heart to embrace the unexpected—to discover the blessing that lies behind the turn in the road. Still a novice at life in many ways, I had a firm hope and expectation that God had great plans for His children, and I was eager to share my anticipation and excitement with other soon-to-be-grads.

Faith Is Healthy!

Belief in God and the practice of faith affects us from the inside out, providing benefits far beyond our mental, emotional, and spiritual health. In his book *The Healing Power of Prayer*, Harold Koenig summarizes over 25 years of research examining the effects of religious beliefs and practices on physical and mental health and well-being. He concludes, "Over 500 studies have now documented correlations between religious practices like prayer and better health. I have also seen the powerful effects of faith in the lives of my patients, and what a tremendous difference prayer has made in their healing—physical, emotional, social, and spiritual. There is power in prayer—there is little doubt about that." The following examples further attest to this:

○ A study conducted in 1999 at the Mid America Heart Institute at St. Luke's Hospital in Kansas City examined nearly 1,000 patients admitted to the coronary care unit of the hospital. Heart patients who had someone praying for them daily, without their knowledge, suffered 10% fewer complications than patients who did not.

○ A Duke University Medical Center study found that people who prayed and attended worship services on a weekly basis were 40% less likely to have high blood pressure than those who lacked an active prayer and worship life.

○ A Stanford University study with over 100 women with metastatic breast cancer found that high levels of religious expression were significantly correlated with higher numbers of natural killer cells, lymphocytes, and other parts of the immune system helpful in destroying cancer cells.

Building Your Spiritual Foundation

My spiritual foundation is built on the knowledge of God's love for me. He had me in mind before the creation of the world. As I grew up, I became aware of my "sinful self"—I did what I didn't want to do and I didn't always do the things I should. My sin separated me from God. God demonstrated His love for me by bridging the gap and becoming man in the person of Jesus Christ. Because Jesus lived, died for my sins, and rose from the dead, my relationship with God was restored.

By faith in Him and through His spirit that lives in me, I can claim victory for my own life. Absolutely nothing has to get the best of me—not fear, anger, jealousy, insecurities, addictions, or pride. I am accepted just as I am; I am forgiven; I am a new creation. He sets my feet on a path toward wholeness and freedom, where I can live abundantly and joyfully.

I had the privilege of growing up with this knowledge and knowing this love as a young person. Yet the truths that I learned only became stronger after the accident:

- God is going with me: "Never will I leave you; never will I forsake you" (Hebrews 13:5).
- God will give me power to meet the challenges of my days: "I can do everything through Him who gives me strength" (Philippians 4:13).
- His power shines through more clearly in my weakness: "My grace is sufficient for you, for My power is made perfect in weakness" (2 Corinthians 12:9).
- He can use both good and bad things for my ultimate benefit: "And we know that in all things God works for the good of those who love Him, who have been called according to His purpose" (Romans 8:28).
- My peace comes from God: "You will keep in perfect peace him whose mind is steadfast, because he trusts in you" (Isaiah 26:3).
- I have new life and the promise of heaven in Him: "For God so loved the world that He gave His one and only son, that whoever believes in Him shall not perish but have eternal life" (John 3:16).

Open Your Life to Living without Limits!

It doesn't matter where you are, where you've been, or what you've done—God's love is available to you today. He wants to do the same for you as He's done for me. Perhaps you've built your foundation on other priorities—your family, your intellect, your job, your material possessions. Perhaps these things have not brought you the security or joy you'd hoped for, and you find yourself still searching. It is not too late to begin building a spiritual foundation today on truths that will never change.

Maybe you attended church or Sunday school in the past. Perhaps you knew about God but never trusted Him with the concerns of your daily life. God has more in mind for you than you can even imagine! You're sitting on a goldmine—the God of the universe wants to impact your life with His love. Imagine the possibilities!

What is your response to this incredible gift? Here are some tools to begin to build or to strengthen your own spiritual foundation:

Read the Bible

The Bible is God's love letter to each of us. In it we have a record of how God has worked with people throughout the course of history and how He wants to impact our lives today. Psalm 119:105 says, "Your word is a lamp to my feet and a light for my path." Who among us wouldn't want light on our path?

Connect with People of Faith

God never intended for us to go through life alone! It is in relationship with others that He teaches and touches us, revealing His love. Seek out a church home, a community of believers with whom you feel comfortable. My involvement in Bible Study Fellowship, Stephens Ministry, Alpha, and disability ministry has greatly strengthened my faith and brought about significant growth through connection with other believers. For some, finding a spiritual mentor or counselor can offer new and different insights. Find a pastor, Sunday school teacher, Bible study leader, or a mature Christian friend to challenge and motivate you on your journey, pointing the way to deeper faith.

Make an "Appointment with the King!"

The summer after my accident, I had a childhood friend and roommate at Fair Hills Resort, Susan Huemann, who challenged me to deepen my personal relationship with God. I remember her saying that if we have a relationship with God but don't spend any time in that relationship, how will it grow? That summer I started my own daily quiet time with a simple prayer list. Family, friends, job, school, my future, relationships, and other daily concerns all found their way on the list, and I prayed over each in turn. That prayer list developed into a prayer journal, which I keep to this day. Together with a daily devotional and reading from the Bible, these components help to start my day with excitement, anticipation, strength, and divine direction. Noted Christian speaker Becky Tirabassi calls it, "An appointment with the King!"

Serve Others

It is in serving others—without expecting anything in return—that we grow and mature in faith; we are empowered when we see a need and ask God to use us to fill it. The inevitable result is that we will get back so much more than we give. When we serve, we model Christ and fulfill His command: "Whatever you did for one of the least of these brothers of mine, you did for Me" (Matthew 25:40).

Exercise Your Unique Gifts

God has given each of us talents and gifts that make a special place for us in the world and in the lives of others. What sets you apart from others? What can you offer the world? Your community? Your church? Your neighbors? 25 years ago, I wrote in my journal to God about the life I hoped to lead:

February 2, 1978

Today in history class we talked about what we want to be if we could be anything in the world. I said that I didn't know what I wanted to be but I want to be really super happy and I always want to show my happiness and love for people in everything I do—meaning: I want to serve You and Your people, God, the best I can, with the love you give me. Because that love is the true, deepest, and most honest love that there is—a genuine love. Thank you God for giving me this genuine love, and please help me, in turn, to give it to others. Thank you for your strength and guidance, God. Amen.

25 years later, I realize He answered that prayer in greater ways than I could ever have possibly imagined. Back then, I never would have imagined that I would be a two-time Paralympian...that I would have the opportunity to deliver wheelchairs to Romania...that I would be a national record-holder...that I would have the opportunity to share God's love with thousands of people each year from a wheelchair and crutches.

When I prayed that teenage prayer, I never would have imagined the course my life would take, that my striving for independence as a quadriplegic would actually lead me to greater dependence upon God. But today I can say, "Thank you, God, for this wheelchair and for the struggle to walk," because through these challenges God has shown me what life is really all about.

Life is not about walking, having the perfect family, a great job, the ideal home, or the right friends. It is about knowing God and living out His plan and purpose for my life...a plan that is more fulfilling, more complex, and more filled with beauty and passion than I ever dreamed possible.

Through my faith and trust in God, I am experiencing His power in miraculous ways, pulling me through the toughest times and enabling me to live a life of purpose, joy, power, vision, and impact...in other words, a life without limits.

> *"Now to Him who is able to do immeasurably more*
> *than all we can ask or imagine, according to*
> *His power that is at work within us, to Him be*
> *glory in the church and in Christ Jesus throughout*
> *all generations for ever and ever! Amen."*
> *Ephesians 3:20-21*

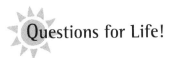

Questions for Life!

1. Do you live with purpose? What is that purpose?
2. How can you feed your faith?

Digging Deeper: Study Guide and Small Group Questions

T his section is designed for readers who wish to take the principles found in *Living without Limits: 10 Keys to Unlocking the Champion in You* and apply them specifically and intentionally in their own lives. Through in-depth questions, this guide will enable you to examine your own life strategies, identify areas of potential growth, and strengthen your body and mind to reach beyond your perceived limitations. You can achieve the dreams in your heart!

Specific scripture passages from the Bible have been included for your consideration and encouragement as you work through "Digging Deeper." These passages uncover rich truths about ourselves and our Creator and will provide you with strength beyond yourself for the journey you are about to embark on.

This section can be used individually for personal reflection or in a small group setting. It is offered with a sincere prayer that through this deeper study, you will be empowered to remove the obstacles before you, unlock your potential, and discover the joy of living without limits!

Chapter 1: The Game Begins

1. Reflect on your childhood. Who were the significant influencers in your life and family?
2. What activities were you involved in that helped to shape your identity?
3. How did you have fun as a child?
4. Was faith in God part of your family life?
5. Describe a turning point in your life.

Food for thought from God's Word:

"For you created my inmost being; you knit me together in my mother's womb. I praise you because I am fearfully and wonderfully made; your works are wonderful, I know that full well" (Psalm 139:13-14).

"For I know the plans I have for you," declares the Lord, "plans to prosper you and not to harm you, plans to give you hope and a future" (Jeremiah 29:11).

"How great is the love the Father has lavished on us, that we should be called children of God! And that is what we are!" (I John 3:1)

Chapter 2: Meet Life Fully!

1. What does venturing look like to you?
2. Identify a time when you dared to risk. Why did you do so? Looking back, are you glad you did?
3. Are you "staying in the game" or have you dropped out? If you're still in the game, what can you do to play better? If you've dropped out, how can you get back in the game?
4. Do you live with expectancy? What does this mean to you? Who do you know who lives with expectancy?

5. Has something happened in your life to cause or force you to repaint your life picture?

Food for Thought from God's Word:

"Be strong and courageous. Do not be terrified; do not be discouraged, the Lord your God will be with you wherever you go" (Joshua 1:9).

"When I am afraid, I will trust in you. In God, whose word I praise, in God I trust; I will not be afraid" (Psalms 56:3-4).

"Though I walk in the midst of trouble, you preserve my life; you stretch out your hand against the anger of my foes, with your right hand you save me" (Psalms 138:7).

"I have come that they may have life, and have it to the full" (John 10:10).

"So we say with confidence, "The Lord is my helper; I will not be afraid. What can man do to me?" (Hebrews 13:6)

Chapter 3: Let Go of Stress

1. What is your natural coping style? Is this an effective way of dealing with stress?
2. Which stress buster is your favorite? Which stress busters do your friends or family use? Is there a new stress buster you would like to try?
3. Do you find that venting helps you to deal with stress? How or to whom do you typically vent?
4. Identify a time when your self-perception limited or enhanced your performance in a situation.
5. Do you have an acute stressor today? What is some "eustress" you experience in your life?

Food for Thought from God's Word:

"Therefore I tell you, do not worry about your life, what you will eat or drink; or about your body, what you will wear. Is not life more important than food, and the body more important than clothes? Look at the birds of the air; they do not sow or reap or stow away in barns, and yet your heavenly father feeds them. Are you not much more valuable than they? Who of you by worrying can add a single hour to his life?" (Matthew 6:25-27)

"Come to me, all who are weary and burdened, and I will give you rest. Take my yoke upon you and learn from me, for I am gentle and humble in heart, and you will find rest for your souls. For my yoke is easy and my burden is light" (Matthew 11:28-30).

"Peace I leave with you; My peace I give you. I do not give to you as the world gives. Do not let your hearts be troubled and do not be afraid" (John 14:27).

"Do not be anxious about anything, but in everything, by prayer and petition, with thanksgiving, present your requests to God. And the peace of God, which transcends all understanding, will guard your hearts and your minds in Christ Jesus" (Philippians 4:6-7).

"Cast all your anxiety on Him because He cares for you" (1 Peter 5:7).

Chapter 4: Cultivate an Attitude of Impact

1. How can you use your attitude to impact others in a positive way?
2. Is giving thanks a part of your life? How can you use gratitude to change your perspective?
3. What are you feeding your mind through your choice of TV shows, music, books, the Internet, and the people with

whom you spend time? Is it positive? How does it effect your attitude about yourself and others?

4. Identify a life situation that brings out a negative attitude in you. What positive affirmations can you use to help transform your thoughts about that situation?
5. Identify a situation where a positive attitude led to a positive result.

Food for Thought from God's Word:

"Do not conform any longer to the pattern of this world, but be transformed by the renewing of your mind. Then you will be able to test and approve what God's will is—His good, pleasing and perfect will" (Romans 12:2).

"Finally, brothers, whatever is true, whatever is noble, whatever is right, whatever is pure, whatever is lovely, whatever is admirable— if anything is excellent or praiseworthy—think about such things" (Philippians 4:8).

"I can do everything through him who gives me strength" (Philippians 4:13).

"Set your heart on things above, not on earthly things" (Colossians 3:2).

"Be joyful always; pray continually; give thanks in all circumstances, for this is God's will for you in Christ Jesus" (1 Thessalonians 5:16-18).

Chapter 5: Make Each Day a Masterpiece

1. What multiple roles do you play in life? What tools can you use to balance those roles so that none of them dominate your life at the expense of others?

2. What does living life fully mean to you? What changes can you implement to make every day a masterpiece?
3. How can you make it easier for yourself to live in the moment, rather than the past or future, and be fully present?
4. Do you have "time boundaries" that allow you to refresh yourself on a daily or weekly basis? How do you refresh yourself mentally, emotionally, and spiritually?
5. Did you give 100% today? Do you every day? Most days? Seldom? How can you improve on your average?

Food for Thought from God's Word:

"This is the day the Lord has made; let us rejoice and be glad in it" (Psalms 118:24).

"Give us today our daily bread" (Matthew 6:11).

"...inwardly we are being renewed day by day" (2 Corinthians 4:16).

"Be very careful, then, how you live—not as unwise but as wise, making the most of every opportunity..." (Ephesians 5:15-16).

"Therefore do not worry about tomorrow, for tomorrow will worry about itself. Each day has enough trouble of its own" (Matthew 6:34).

Chapter 6: Strengthen Your Mind

1. What is a present-day situation where additional information could empower you or offer you an insight to move forward?
2. When has sharing information about yourself broken down barriers between you and another person?

3. As you look back over your life, when have detours ended up as blessings?

4. Identify a situation when you have experienced personal growth or healing after gathering information. What might have happened if you had not gathered that information?

5. How has knowledge you have gained from life experiences equipped you to serve others?

Food for Thought from God's Word:

"You guide me with your counsel, and afterward you will take me into glory" (Psalm 73:24).

"The fear of the Lord is the beginning of knowledge, but fools despise wisdom and discipline" (Proverbs 1:7).

"The Holy Spirit will teach you at that time what you should say" (Luke 12:12).

"Do not merely listen to the word, and so deceive yourselves. Do what it says" (James 1:22).

"...faith by itself, if it is not accompanied by action, is dead" (James 2:17).

Chapter 7: Set Goals

1. What is one goal you have achieved and what steps did you take to make it possible?

2. What are some obstacles you've had to overcome to reach your goals?

3. Who are the goal setters in your life? If there isn't one, how can you find one?

4. When it comes to committing to a goal, are you a cop-out, a holdout, a dropout, or an all-out?

5.   What is an area of your life where you would like a change?
     Set a goal and begin today!

Food for Thought from God's Word:

"So we make it our goal to please him, whether we are at home in the body or away from it" (2 Corinthians 5:9).

"Forgetting what is behind and straining toward what is ahead, I press on toward the goal to win the prize for which God has called me heavenward in Christ Jesus" (Philippians 3:13-14).

"For God did not give us a spirit of timidity, but a spirit of power, of love and of self-discipline" (2 Timothy 1:7).

"Therefore, since we are surrounded by such a great cloud of witnesses, let us throw off everything that hinders and the sin that so easily entangles, and let us run with perseverance the race marked out for us" (Hebrews 12:1).

"Therefore, prepare your minds for action; be self-controlled; set your hope fully on the grace to be given you when Jesus Christ is revealed" (1 Peter 1:13).

Chapter 8: Create a Circle of Support

1.   Identify your circles of support, both past and present. How have they changed over the years?
2.   Share a time in your life when you felt like you were all alone. What did you do?
3.   Describe a situation when a friendship was a strength for you during a challenging time. When have you been a support for someone else?
4.   Describe a friendship that has expanded your world or been instrumental in helping you reach your dreams.

5. Do you need to expand your support system? What can you do today to get started?

Food for Thought from God's Word:

"Again, I tell you that if two of you on earth agree about anything you ask for, it will done for you by my father in heaven. For where two or three come together in my name, there am I with them" (Matthew 18:19-20).

"Carry each other's burdens, and in this way you will fulfill the law of Christ" (Galatians 6:2).

"Be kind and compassionate to one another, forgiving each other, just as in Christ God forgave you" (Ephesians 4:32).

"But encourage one another daily..." (Hebrews 3:13).

"Let us not give up meeting together, as some are in the habit of doing, but let us encourage one another..." (Hebrews 10:25).

Chapter 9: Increase Your Energy

1. Are you an energetic person? A lethargic person? Somewhere in the middle? To what do you attribute your energy level?
2. Identify people in your life who can help you on your journey to better health.
3. Are there any preconceived inadequacies or limitations keeping you out of the game?
4. What is your definition of success regarding your health or fitness? Do you need to redefine your concept of success to stay in the game?
5. What is the first step you can take towards better health and improved energy today?

Food for Thought from God's Word:

"By the seventh day God had finished the work He had been doing; so on the seventh day He rested from all His work" (Genesis 2:2).

"Everything is permissible for me"—but not everything is beneficial. "Everything is permissible for me"—but I will not be mastered by anything (1 Corinthians 6:12).

"...your body is a temple of the Holy Spirit...honor God with your body" (1 Corinthians 6:19-20).

"So whether you eat or drink or whatever you do, do it all for the glory of God" (1 Corinthians 10:31).

"I can do everything through him who gives me strength" (Philippians 4:13).

Chapter 10: Embrace Humor!

1. Reflect back on your childhood and family of origin. How was humor expressed in your home? How do you use humor in your family life today?
2. What is an embarrassing moment in your life? Can you look back on it now and laugh?
3. Identify a situation where humor broke the tension or helped people to bond in a stressful time.
4. Name a person who makes you laugh. How does it feel to be with that person?
5. What can you do today to bring more laughter into your life today?

Food for Thought from God's Word:

"A happy heart makes the face cheerful, but heartache crushes the spirit" (Proverbs 15:13).

"A cheerful heart is good medicine, but a crushed spirit dries up the bones" (Proverbs 17:22).

"There is a time for everything and a season for every activity under heaven: a time to weep and a time to laugh, a time to mourn and a time to dance..." (Ecclesiastes 3:1, 4).

"I've told you this so that my joy may be in you and that your joy may be complete" (John 15:11).

"Be joyful always..." (1 Thessalonians 5:16).

Chapter 11: Build a Spiritual Foundation

1. What factors have shaped your belief system?
2. What person of faith has impacted your life?
3. Has your faith ever been a comfort to you during a difficult time?
4. Discuss your answers to the statements on page 154 regarding your purpose and the gifts God has given you.
5. Do you desire to grow in your relationship with God? What is one step you can take today toward strengthening or building your spiritual foundation?

Food for Thought from God's Word:

"...choose for yourselves this day whom you will serve..." (Joshua 24:15).

"...I have come that they may have life, and have it to the full" (John 10:10).

"But thanks be to God! He gives us the victory through our Lord Jesus Christ" (1 Corinthians 15:57).

"Jesus answered, "I am the way and the truth and the life. No one comes to the Father except through me" (John 14:6).

"He will wipe every tear from their eyes. There will be no more death or mourning or crying or pain, for the old order of things has passed away" (Revelation 21:4-5).

About the Author

Judy Siegle is a masters prepared social worker on staff at MeritCare Health System in Fargo, ND as a Community Relations Specialist. A two-time Paralympian and national record holder, she is highly sought after as a professional speaker and workshop leader. For more information on Judy, visit her website at www.judysiegle.com or write to: Judy Siegle, MeritCare Health System, PO Box MC, Fargo, ND 58122.